Kids'
Guide to
American History

Interior design and layout by Thinkpen Design

Published by Barbour Publishing, Inc., P.O. Box 719, Uhrichsville, Ohio 44683, www.barbourbooks.com

Our mission is to publish and distribute inspirational products offering exceptional value and biblical encouragement to the masses.

Printed in the United States of America.
Courier Kendallville, Inc. Kendallville, IN 46755, August 2012, D10003473

KiDS' Guide to American History

WHO, WHAT, WHEN, WHERE, WHY—
FROM A CHRISTIAN PERSPECTIVE

BY TRACY M. SUMNER

BARBOUR
PUBLISHING

WHAT'S IN THIS BOOK

Have you ever sat in your social studies or history class at school, wishing you knew more about how the United States came to be the country it is today? If you have, then this book is for you! (If you haven't, it's still a pretty cool book anyway.)

As you read through this book, you'll learn the basics of US history, starting with European explorations of North America that started as far back as about 1,000 years ago. You'll also learn about the brave people who started coming here from Europe about four centuries ago and began setting up 13 communities called *colonies*. You'll also learn the exciting story of how those colonies eventually became the original 13 states of the United States of America.

If that's not enough—and we hope it won't be!—you'll also learn about how Americans began moving west from the original 13 colonies to explore and settle the rest of the country.

And, of course, you'll learn that many of the people who played important parts in American history were people who believed in God and believed that He had a purpose in allowing the United States of America to get its start *and* expand to become the nation you live in today.

But there's even more! This book also includes fun and informative features with facts, figures, and profiles of important people in American history. Here is a list of those features:

Historic Happenings:
Events in American history that are worth remembering

History Makers: Stories about
important people in American history and the things they did to become famous

Worth Repeating: Interesting
things that people in the past said about America

Interesting!: Good-to-know facts
about the people, places, and events in the history of the United States

Before you get started, here are some things to keep in mind:

First of all, this book won't teach you everything there is to know about US history. Entire books have been written about many of these important people and events, and it wasn't easy deciding what to include and what to leave out.

Our hope is that this book will give you a good idea of how the United States started and grew to become the great nation it is today. Then, through your own studies, you can build on what you've learned. You will also have a great head start when you study American history at school!

Second (and this is kind of a warning), some of the things that have happened in our country aren't very pleasant to read or think about. There have been several big wars, and a lot of people died to protect our freedom. You'll also find some stories about people who went through some really hard times—and some who even died because they didn't have enough to eat or because they got sick. And because people aren't perfect, you'll read about some of the mistakes the United States made along the way.

About now, you might be thinking, *Why would I want to read about wars and about people suffering and dying? That doesn't sound like fun to me.* Look at it this way: If you understand what some people had to give up in order to build such a great nation as the United States, it will make you more thankful for the freedom we have today.

When you're finished reading this book, you won't know everything there is to know about American history. But you'll understand most of the important events and how a lot of people had to depend on God, be brave, and not give up in order to make the United States of America the great nation it is today.

And maybe—*just maybe*—you'll find that learning about history is not only interesting but a lot of fun, too!

CHAPTER 1

A Time of "New World" Discovery

The Pre-Colonial Period of American History

If you could travel back in time to see what the United States looked like 500 or 600 years ago, what do you think you'd find? Obviously, it wouldn't look anything like it does today. There were no cities or roads back then, and the only people you would see were the Native Americans—which some people call Indians—who had lived here for generations.

In those days, most of our ancestors were living in Europe, Asia, or Africa, and they didn't know much about the unexplored territory that would come to be known as the New World. In fact, very few of them even knew it existed!

But that began to change toward the end of the fifteenth century (the 1400s) when brave and curious men like Christopher Columbus, John Cabot, Ponce de León, and many others started sailing west in search of discovery.

There was a huge "New World" out there for the European explorers to discover.

Christopher Columbus Sails West

**In fourteen hundred and ninety-two,
Columbus sailed the ocean blue.**

That little poem probably helps you remember that way back in 1492, an Italian sailor named Christopher Columbus set sail from Spain and eventually landed on some islands near two big continents that would come to be known as "the Americas" (North America, which is where the United States, Canada, and Mexico are located; and South America, which today has 12 countries, including Brazil, Argentina, Peru, and Chile).

What you might not know is that Columbus's real claim to fame is that he discovered the Americas *by accident*. In fact, he wasn't even trying to discover anything—except an easier, safer way for sailors back then to travel to India.

Christopher Columbus was born in the Republic of Genoa in northwestern Italy in 1451. His father was Domenico Colombo (*Columbus* is the English spelling of the Italian name Colombo), who made a living for his family by working as a wool weaver. He also owned a cheese stand, which young Christopher helped run. Christopher's mother was Susanna Fontanarossa, and he had three brothers—Bartolomeo, Giovanni Pellegrino, and Giacomo—and a sister, Bianchinetta.

Christopher Columbus didn't get much of an education when he was young. Instead of studying, he began sailing. He traveled around the Mediterranean Sea and even traveled as far as England and Ireland. When Columbus was about 25 years old, he was shipwrecked and made his way ashore in Portugal. He later lived there with his brother Bartolomeo.

Finding a New Way to India

Like other sailors in his day, Columbus knew that traveling around the southern tip of Africa to reach India was very dangerous and difficult. Not only that, it took a long time! He believed he could find a new route to India by sailing west across the Atlantic Ocean. He didn't know there were two big continents in the way (that would one day be called the Americas). He thought if he just sailed west, he would circle the globe and eventually end up in eastern Asia.

Columbus spent seven years traveling across Europe looking for someone to support his mission to find a new way to India, but no one wanted to help him. In fact, most of the kings and queens of Europe made

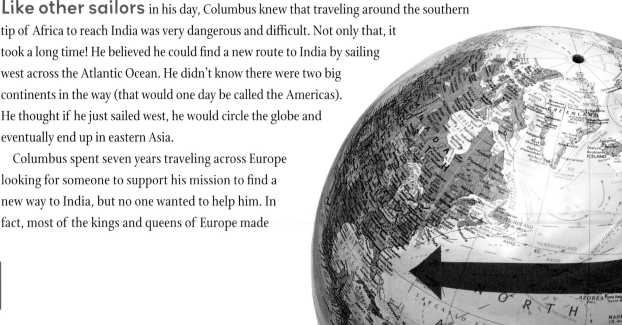

fun of him and told him it was too dangerous to try to sail around the world.

But Columbus didn't give up. He traveled to Spain looking for support. The Spanish king, Ferdinand, and his queen, Isabella, wanted to prove that Spain

could be just as powerful and successful as its neighbor, Portugal. So in August 1492, they granted Christopher Columbus the supplies, men, and ships that he needed for his trip. The three ships the king and queen gave Columbus were named the *Niña*, the *Pinta*, and the *Santa Maria*.

Time to Set Sail!

On August 3, 1492, Columbus and his men set sail from Palos, Spain. Columbus thought the journey would take only four weeks. But after more than two months at sea without spotting land, Columbus's men began to worry that they would be lost and would starve to death (and they had no idea where they were). On October 10, the other sailors began to turn against Columbus, so he made a deal with them: If they didn't find land within three days, they would turn around and head home.

It looked like Columbus's voyage might turn out to be a waste of time; but on October 12, 1492, one of the sailors spotted land. Columbus didn't know it at the time, but what he and his crew had discovered was an island in the Caribbean Sea.

INTERESTING!

One of the myths about Christopher Columbus (one you might even have read in one of your school textbooks) was that no one believed him when he said the world was round and not flat. But people living during Columbus's time—at least the people with some education—knew very well that the earth was round. A few centuries before the birth of Jesus, Greek scientists and philosophers already knew that the earth was round. In fact, around 200 BC, a Greek scholar named Eratosthenes of Cyrene had already figured out pretty accurately the distance around the world.

WORTH REPEATING

"It was the Lord who put into my mind (I could feel His hand upon me) that fact that it would be possible to sail from here to the Indies. All who heard of my project rejected it with laughter, ridiculing me. There is no question that the inspiration was from the Holy Spirit, because He comforted me with rays of marvelous inspiration from the Holy Scriptures."
—Christopher Columbus

Columbus named the newly discovered island San Salvador, but when he went ashore the next morning, he found that the people already living there called it Guanahani. Columbus met with some of the natives and traded with them. He stayed on the island for two days before setting sail again. He stopped at three other islands in the Bahamas—which he named Santa Maria de la Concepción, Fernandina, and Isabella—before landing at Bariay Bay, Cuba, on October 28.

Columbus spent the last few days of October and all of November exploring the island of Cuba. While there, he looked for gold (he didn't find any) and for Chinese civilizations he had read about (he still didn't know he wasn't in Asia). On December 5, 1492, Columbus arrived at another island, which he named Hispaniola. Today, that island is where you'll find the nations of Haiti and the Dominican Republic.

On January 16, 1493, Columbus departed Hispaniola for the return trip to Spain. The *Niña* and the *Pinta* arrived in Palos, Spain, on March 15. Over the next several years, Columbus returned three more times to Cuba and Hispaniola, and he also visited places like modern-day Trinidad and Nicaragua.

It might sound funny now, but on Columbus's first voyage, he had no idea where he had landed. He had sailed almost all the way across the Atlantic Ocean, just as he had planned, but instead of reaching India, he landed in a place that no one from Europe knew existed. What's even more amazing is that Columbus never knew he hadn't reached India. In fact, by the time he died in 1506, he still didn't realize what he had discovered.

Columbus: A Man of Faith

You probably won't read about it in your school textbooks, but Christopher Columbus was a devout Christian who read his Bible and prayed regularly. Like any other European explorer during the pre-colonial period, Columbus had a desire to find new places and better ways to reach those places. But he also had a strong desire to tell people in other nations about Jesus. He especially wanted to take this message to people in eastern Asia.

After landing at the island he named San Salvador, Columbus wrote about his experiences with the natives who lived there: "As I saw that they were very friendly to us, and perceived that they could be much more easily converted to our holy faith by gentle means than by force, I presented them with some red caps, and strings of beads to wear upon the neck, and many other trifles of small value, wherewith they were much delighted and became wonderfully attached to us. I am of opinion that they would very readily become Christians, as they appear to have no religion."

John Cabot: North America's Real Discoverer

Before the beginning of the sixteenth century (the 1500s), Spain and Portugal did most of the exploring of the New World. But in 1497, King Henry VII of England sent an Italian explorer named John Cabot (Giovanni Caboto in Italian) to check out what Columbus had recently found.

Cabot explored what is now Newfoundland and Nova Scotia in Canada, as well as the area now known as New England in the United States. Even though another century would pass before England established a permanent colony in the New World, Cabot claimed those lands for England. Historians believe Cabot was the first European explorer to travel to the continent of North America since the early eleventh century.

How America Became "America"

Not long after Christopher Columbus died in 1506, people began to realize that what he had discovered was not a new route to India, but a completely different part of the world. The first person to make that suggestion was an Italian explorer named Amerigo Vespucci (1454–1512).

Vespucci grew up in Florence, Italy. He enjoyed reading and collected a lot of books and maps. As a young man, he began working for bankers in Florence, and in 1492 he traveled to Spain to take care of business for his employer. While he was in Spain, he began working on ships. In 1499, he sailed with a crew to South America and saw the mouth of the Amazon River.

Vespucci made at least one more trip (probably two) across the Atlantic Ocean before he died of malaria (a disease often carried by mosquitoes) on February 22, 1512. He is remembered as the man who realized that the land that would later be known as America was not part of eastern Asia, as Columbus had believed, but a newly discovered continent. Vespucci is also remembered as the man this new continent was named after.

That happened around 1507, when a German preacher and mapmaker named Martin Wardseemüller printed a map of the known world with the name "America" printed across the South American continent. Wardseemüller had read of Amerigo Vespucci's travels to the New World, and he wanted to honor the Italian explorer by naming the newly discovered continent after him.

A few years later, Wardseemüller changed his mind about the name of Vespucci's New World discovery. But by then it was too late. He had already printed thousands of copies of his map and sold them to people all across Europe. Wardseemüller couldn't change the fact that everyone in Europe called the New World "America."

In 1538 a European mapmaker named Gerardus Mercator developed the first world map to include the continents of North America and South America. So even though Amerigo Vespucci wasn't one of the most important explorers to see the New World, his name became famous.

This turret is a much-photographed part of Puerto Rico's Morro Castle, begun about 30 years after Ponce de León became governor of the island.

Ponce de León: Picking up Where Columbus Left Off

Juan Ponce de León was a sailor who accompanied Christopher Columbus on his voyage to the New World in 1493. When Columbus returned to Europe, Ponce de León decided to stay in Hispaniola.

In 1508 Spain appointed Ponce de León governor of a nearby island called Boriquien (modern-day Puerto Rico). Legend has it that while Ponce de León was in Boriquien, he heard the natives' stories about a magical source of water called the Fountain of Youth. Supposedly, drinking water from the fountain made a person young again. According to legend, Ponce de León spent a few years trying to find out where the Fountain of Youth was. When he was told it was on an island called Bimini, he organized an expedition to go search for it.

Many historians doubt the accuracy of the Fountain of Youth story. But early in 1513, Ponce de León received permission from Spain to set sail from Boriquien. He loaded three ships—the *Santiago*, the *San Cristobal* and the *Santa Maria de la Consolacion*—with at least 200 men, and on March 4, 1513, they set sail.

Ponce de León's expedition sailed for several days and didn't find Bimini; but on March 27, they came within sight of what they thought was a large island (but was actually a long peninsula connected to North America). Sometime in early April 1513, Ponce de León became the first European known to have set foot on what is now the state of Florida. He named the area in honor of Spain's Easter celebration called *Pascua Florida*, which means "Feast of Flowers."

Ponce de León eventually returned to Boriquien, where he continued as governor, but in 1521 he began another voyage to Florida. This time, he was accompanied by about 200 people. They took with them about 50 horses, other livestock, and farming equipment, because they wanted to start a colony on the peninsula.

The expedition landed on the southwest coast of Florida and started to build a settlement. As the men worked to build houses, they were attacked by native tribesmen. Many of Ponce de León's men died in the attack, and he was wounded. The survivors boarded their ship and sailed to Cuba, where Ponce de León died of his wounds in July 1521.

Catching the Exploration Bug

The expeditions of Christopher Columbus, Juan Ponce de León, and John Cabot were just the beginning of European exploration of the New World. Before many more years had passed, explorers from several European nations boarded ships and headed west. Some of these explorers went looking for gold and other riches, while others just wanted to find out what these new lands might have to offer them and their people. By the one hundredth anniversary of Columbus's unintended voyage to the New World, dozens of other Europeans had embarked on explorations of their own.

Here is a list of some of those explorers and what they found:

- In 1519 a Spanish explorer and mapmaker named **Alonso de Pineda** (1494–1520) led several expeditions to map the western coastlines of the Gulf of Mexico. His map is believed to be the first document in the history of what later became the state of Texas. It is also the first map of the Gulf Coast region of the United States.

- In 1524 an Italian explorer named **Giovanni da Verrazano** (1485–1528), who was sailing for France, explored the east coast of North America, from Cape Fear (modern-day North Carolina) north to Nova Scotia. Along the way, he also discovered New York Harbor.

- In 1528 a Spanish explorer named **Alvar Cabeza de Vaca** (about 1488–about 1557) explored the territory that later became the states of Texas, Arizona, and New Mexico, as well as parts of northeastern Mexico.

- In 1534 a French explorer named **Jacques Cartier** (1491–1557) explored the Great Lakes area and the Saint Lawrence River. He was the first European to map the Gulf of Saint Lawrence and the shores of the Saint Lawrence River. Cartier claimed the area for France.

The Verrazano-Narrows Bridge, connecting the New York City boroughs of Staten Island and Brooklyn, was named for the Italian explorer who was the first European to sail into New York Harbor.

- On May 30, 1539, a Spanish explorer named **Hernando de Soto** (about 1500–1542) arrived on the west coast of Florida. He and his men were looking for gold and silver, and they explored much of southeastern North America. De Soto and his men camped for five months near what is now the city of

Tallahassee, Florida. De Soto died near the Mississippi River in 1542, but other members of his expedition eventually arrived in Mexico.

- In 1540 a Spanish conquistador (conqueror) named **Francisco Vásquez de Coronado** (1510–1554) explored southwestern North America, including what is now New Mexico. Coronado was looking for the mythical Seven Cities of Gold. Coronado also explored the Colorado River and what later became the state of Kansas.

- In 1540 a Spaniard named **Garcia López de Cárdenas** discovered the Grand Canyon.

- In 1542 a Portuguese explorer named **Juan Rodriguez Cabrillo** (about 1499–1543), who was sailing for Spain, explored the west coast of North America. Cabrillo is credited with discovering the coast of California.

- In 1559 a Spanish conquistador named **Tristán de Luna** (1519–1571) was sent on an expedition to conquer Florida. He established a short-lived colony in what is now Pensacola. It was one of the earliest European settlements in North America.

- In 1563 a Spanish explorer named **Francisco de Ibarra** (about 1539–1575) explored what is now New Mexico. He also founded the Mexican city of Durango.

- In 1577 an English sea captain named **Sir Francis Drake** (1544–1596) began his quest to sail completely around the world. He started from Plymouth, England, on December 13, 1577, and returned to the same place on September 26, 1580.

- In 1584 two Englishmen, **Philip Amadas** (1550–1618) and **Arthur Barlowe** (1550–1620), explored the coast of North Carolina. Both men were sailing on behalf of the English explorer Sir Walter Raleigh (about 1554–1618).

- In 1585 **Sir Walter Raleigh** received permission from the king of England to explore and settle in North America. In June of that year, Raleigh established a short-lived colony on Roanoke Island (North Carolina).

- In 1598 a Spaniard named **Juan de Archuleta** explored what is now Colorado.

- In 1609 an English explorer named **Henry Hudson** (about 1565–about 1611), sailing on behalf of the Netherlands, discovered the area that would later become Delaware. Hudson's explorations led to the Dutch colonization of New York and Delaware.

North America's First European Settlement

Florida has come a long way since Spanish adventurers first explored the area. Today, the state is a popular tourist destination—well-known for sites such as Walt Disney World.

In the next chapter, you will read how the colonies that eventually became the first 13 states at one time all belonged to Great Britain. But none of those colonies was the first permanent European settlement established in North America. That honor goes to a place called St. Augustine in northeast Florida.

Pedro Menéndez de Avilés established St. Augustine on orders from King Philip II of Spain, who told him to explore and colonize the territory and to destroy any other European settlements, including a French outpost called Fort Caroline. King Philip also told Menéndez to conquer (but not destroy) the Timucua, the native tribe that lived in the area.

Menéndez's fleet battled through Atlantic storms that claimed several of their ships, but on August 28, 1565, they first sighted land. On September 8—42 years before the first British settlement in North America was established— Menéndez (along with 500 soldiers, 200 sailors, and 100 passengers) established the settlement and named it in honor of St. Augustine of Hippo, a famous Christian writer who lived in the fourth and fifth centuries. Menéndez was also the first governor of Florida.

HISTORY MAKERS

Pánfilo de Narváez (about 1470–1528) was a Spanish explorer and soldier best remembered for helping Spain conquer Cuba in 1511. He also led a Spanish expedition of about 300 men to North America in 1527. The explorers landed on the west coast of Florida (near what is now Tampa Bay) in April 1528. Many of the men died due to hurricanes and battles with the natives, and the rest were stranded when their ship's pilot sailed to Mexico without them. The abandoned men built five rafts and began sailing west toward Mexico. Only two of the rafts made it all the way to safety on Galveston Island (off the coast of Texas). Narváez died during the trip.

Jamestown— Where US History Really Began

By the beginning of the seventeenth century, European explorers had been traveling to North America for quite a long time. But in 1607, settlers from England built the first English settlement in North America, called Jamestown, in what is now Virginia. Even though the United States of America wouldn't be established for another 170 years, Jamestown in many ways was the real start of US history.

The year before the Jamestown settlers arrived, King James I of England (the same King James who authorized a translation of the Bible called the King James Version) gave a group of merchants representing the Virginia Company permission to settle in North America.

King James wanted to establish a settlement in the New World because he wanted to keep up with other European countries that already had colonies there. By that time, Spain had established colonies in South America, Central America, and parts of North America; and France had colonies in what is now eastern Canada.

On December 20, 1606, a party of men and boys boarded the ships *Susan Constant*, *Godspeed*, and *Discovery* and headed out from England. The passengers included carpenters, a blacksmith, a mason, a tailor, a goldsmith, a barber, and two doctors. Captain Christopher Newport was in charge of the expedition.

The Jamestown Landing

On May 14, 1607, 104 colonists landed on the coast of Virginia and began to set up camp. At first they lived in a tent camp, but within a month they completed construction of a large fort on the banks of the James River, which they named after King James I of England. By this time, seven leaders had been appointed: Christopher Newport, John Smith, John Ratcliffe, George Kendall, Edward Maria Wingfield, Bartholomew Gosnold, and John Martin. The council elected Wingfield as the colony's first president.

At first, things didn't go very well for the settlers. The water there made many of them sick, and some men died from their illnesses. They didn't have enough food to eat because many of the men didn't know how to farm or hunt. The summers were far hotter and the winters far colder than they were used to. And if all that wasn't enough, they had to deal with attacks from the Algonquian natives who lived in the area. Just eight months after the landing at Jamestown, only 38 of the original colonists were still alive.

King James I of England—in a painting from about 13 years after the Jamestown settlement was founded.

HISTORY MAKERS

John Ratcliffe was the captain of the *Discovery*, one of the three ships sent to settle the colony at Jamestown. Later, he became the second president of the colony. Ratcliffe died in December 1609 in an attack by Powhatan Indians.

Between January and October 1608, ships carrying several hundred more colonists from England arrived in Jamestown, and they found terrible conditions there. Not only that, a series of events made things even worse. On January 7, 1609, a fire broke out in the Jamestown fort, destroying many of the buildings, including the colony's first church. The fire also destroyed most of their provisions.

In September 1608, the Jamestown leaders elected John Smith as their new president, but Smith immediately had to deal with a bunch of very unhappy colonists. Many of them wanted to go back to England because they had to work so hard just to survive in the New World. Many others were disappointed that they couldn't find any gold in the area around the Jamestown colony.

Things got a lot worse for the Jamestown colonists during the winter of 1609–1610, which came to be known as Starving Time. Hostile natives surrounded the fort, which was already out of food. People who left the fort to try to find food died at the hands of the Native Americans, while the ones who stayed inside starved.

The mysterious word "Croatoan" was found carved in a post at the "Lost Colony" of Jamestown—but none of the more than 100 settlers were ever seen again.

When two ships, *Deliverance* and *Patience*, arrived, the people on board found only 60 starving survivors (out of about 500 colonists) in the ruins of the Jamestown fort.

On June 7 the survivors boarded the *Deliverance* and *Patience*—both of which had been built from the wreckage of a ship called *Sea Venture* that had run aground in a hurricane in Bermuda in July 1609—and got ready to head back to England. It looked like the end of the Jamestown settlement. But the two ships were stopped shortly after they left Jamestown and ordered to return and wait for Lord De La Warr, the newly appointed governor of Virginia, who was on his way with three ships filled with supplies. De La Warr arrived in Jamestown on June 10, 1610—just in time to save the remaining colonists' lives and persuade them not to give up and go home to England.

Jamestown's New "Cash Crop"

The arrival of the *Deliverance* and *Patience* came just at the right time. Not only did the ships carry food and other supplies the few survivors desperately needed, it also brought a man named John Rolfe, whose experiments with tobacco gave the settlement a crop that they could sell back to England and trade with the Native Americans.

Life remained very difficult in Jamestown after Rolfe's arrival. The people in the settlement had tried several ways to support themselves, but none of them had worked. Meanwhile, the Virginia Company kept sending more money and people to try to help.

Rolfe began growing tobacco in Virginia in 1612. The natives had already been growing tobacco there, but the colonists didn't like it. Rolfe planted a variety he had discovered in Bermuda and had sold in large quantities to English merchants.

Around the time Rolfe began growing tobacco in Virginia, he also met Pocahontas, the daughter of Powhatan, the Indian chief who had led his

HISTORY MAKERS

Alexander Whitaker (1585–1616) was a Christian minister who became known as The Apostle of Virginia. In 1611 Whitaker arrived at the Virginia Colony, where he established the first Presbyterian congregation. He also taught the Indian tribes in the area about Jesus and brought many of the natives to the Christian faith. His most famous convert was Pocahontas, who was baptized and given the English name Rebecca. By 1616 there were enough Native American Christians that the Virginia Company built Henrico College, which taught the Indians to read the Bible.

Tobacco remains a money-maker in modern America. Oddly, these tobacco plants are growing in Pennsylvania's Amish Country.

people to attack the colonists. Rolfe first met Pocahontas after some colonists kidnapped her and offered to trade her for English prisoners held by Powhatan. But the trade never happened. Instead, Pocahontas was taken to an English settlement, where she learned English and became a Christian. Rolfe married Pocahontas in the spring of 1614.

Rolfe's experiments with tobacco gave the colonists the cash crop they needed to survive, and that resulted in the growth and expansion of the Virginia Colony. Rolfe's marriage to Pocahontas led to peace between the Indians and colonists, which allowed the settlement to grow. Between 1618 and 1623, thousands of new settlers, hoping to get rich growing and selling tobacco, migrated to Virginia. During that time, the population of the Jamestown settlement grew to about 4,500 people. ❌

THE WEDDING OF POCAHONTAS.
With John Rolf.

CHAPTER 2

The Colonial Era

The Pilgrims, the Puritans,
and Other English Colonists

Between 1607 and 1733, England established 13 colonies on the Atlantic coast of North America. Those colonies were Connecticut, Delaware, Georgia, Maryland, Massachusetts Bay, New Hampshire, New Jersey, New York, North Carolina, Pennsylvania, Rhode Island, South Carolina, and Virginia.

Even though all of these colonies belonged to England, each developed its own government, economy, and way of life. As you'll see, life was difficult at first for the people who lived in these colonies. But they kept their faith in God, kept working hard, and eventually established the first 13 states of the United States of America.

Who Were the Pilgrims?

By the early seventeenth century, many Christians in England were unhappy with the Church of England. During a historic event in the sixteenth century called the Protestant Reformation, the Church of England had broken away from the Catholic Church and made a lot of changes.

For some Christians though, the changes in the Church of England, the country's official church at the time, didn't go far enough. One group of Christians who were most unhappy with the Church of England was the Pilgrims. (They were also called Separatists because they wanted to separate from the Church of England.)

Another group of Christians who were unhappy with the church were the Puritans. The Puritans wanted the Church of England to stop using some of the practices used by the Catholic Church and to start worshipping God the way they believed the Bible said to do it. They were called Puritans because they wanted to *purify* the Church of England from all the influences of the Catholic Church.

The Pilgrims were different from the Puritans because they didn't believe the Church of England would ever change. The Pilgrims gave up hope after King James I refused to allow them to conduct their worship services the way they believed the Bible instructed them. Not only that, but King James said that all church congregations—

WHAT THE MAYFLOWER COMPACT SAID

In the name of God, Amen. We, whose names are under-written, the loyal subjects of our dread sovereign Lord, King James, by the grace of God, of Great Britain, France, and Ireland, King, Defender of the Faith, etc.

Having undertaken, for the glory of God, and advancement of the Christian faith, and honor of our King and Country, a voyage to plant the first colony in the northern parts of Virginia; do by these presents, solemnly and mutually in the presence of God and one of another, covenant and combine ourselves together into a civil body politic, for our better ordering and preservation, and furtherance of the ends aforesaid; And by virtue hereof to enact, constitute, and frame, such just and equal laws, ordinances, acts, constitutions and offices, from time to time, as shall be thought most meet and convenient for the general good of the Colony; unto which we promise all due submission and obedience. In witness whereof we have hereunto subscribed our names at Cape Cod the eleventh of November, in the reign of our sovereign Lord, King James, of England, France, and Ireland, the eighteenth, and of Scotland the fifty-fourth. Anno Domini, 1620.

including the Puritans—must run their services the way the Church of England told them to (or it would lead to the death penalty). The Pilgrims decided that their only choice was to leave England.

Off to the New World. . . But First. . .

At first, a group of Separatists left England and traveled to Holland, where they stayed for several years. But soon they decided to leave Holland because they wanted their children to grow up English, not Dutch. They knew England had claimed territories in North America, so they made plans to sail across the Atlantic Ocean and start a colony.

After a difficult time of negotiations with the Virginia Company of London, the Pilgrims were given some land in North America. On September 6, 1620, a group of about 100 Pilgrims boarded the *Mayflower*, a 180-ton sailing ship, and set sail from Plymouth, England. About two months later, they landed near what is now Cape Cod, Massachusetts. The people on the *Mayflower* had intended to sail to the mouth of the Hudson River, but the leaders of the voyage decided to land farther north.

Not all of the colonists traveling on the *Mayflower* were members of the congregation that was starting the new colony. When the *Mayflower* landed in Massachusetts instead of New York, the agreed-upon landing spot,

some of the people declared that no one on the ship could tell them what to do. In response to this minor rebellion, the leaders on the *Mayflower* wrote a now-famous document called the Mayflower Compact, which said that everyone would agree to cooperate and do what was best for the new colony. On November 11, 1620, with the *Mayflower* anchored in the harbor at Cape Cod, 41 of the ship's passengers—all men—signed the Mayflower Compact, which established the laws that everyone in the new colony had to follow.

That same day, the *Mayflower* finally landed at Plymouth, where they would soon face a terrible first winter as colonists in the New World. A man named John Carver, who had worked to charter the *Mayflower*, and who was one of the most respected members of the group, was chosen the first governor of the Plymouth Colony.

The Pilgrims' first year at Plymouth was very difficult. Nearly half the settlers died of disease. But life slowly and steadily began to improve for the people who survived. The Pilgrims were able to make peace with the Indian tribes around them, which allowed them to begin making a living through farming, fishing, and trading with other people. No one got rich farming or fishing, but those pursuits allowed the people to take care of themselves without help from England after only five years.

The Massachusetts Bay Colony

In 1630, about 10 years after the Pilgrims left Holland to form the Plymouth Colony, another group—the Puritans—left England to start a new colony in North America. They also came to what is now the state of Massachusetts, and they started a settlement called the Massachusetts Bay Colony.

Like the Pilgrims, the Puritans wanted to be able to worship God without interference from the Church of England. At first, the Puritans wanted to "purify" the Church of England from within. The English government didn't want the church to change, so it treated

HISTORIC HAPPENINGS

Life was not easy for the Puritans living in Massachusetts during the colonial period. Probably the worst calamity the colonists faced was King Philip's War, which has also been called Metacom's Rebellion. It was a conflict between American Indians and inhabitants of the southern part of the New England colonies. It was named after Metacomet, the Native American leader, whom the English called King Philip. In April 1678, nearly two years after Metacomet died in battle, the war ended with the signing of a treaty at Casco Bay. Nearly half of the area's towns were destroyed, and its economy was nearly ruined. Many colonists died, including 10 percent of the men available to fight.

many Puritans very badly because of their beliefs and practices. Many Puritans died for what they believed in, and many more lost their businesses and homes.

One group of Puritans wanted to move away from England to live in a place where they could practice their religion without government interference or persecution. In 1629 England's new king, Charles I, issued a document called a charter, which gave the Puritans permission to move to North America and begin living and doing business there. This group of more than 1,000 Puritans was called the Massachusetts Bay Company, and its leader was John Winthrop.

In 1620 the Puritans of the Massachusetts Bay Company packed up their belongings and sailed for the New World. They landed near what is now Salem, Massachusetts, but they quickly moved to an area that is now part of Boston. The Puritans set up their own government and passed their own laws.

The first two years in the new settlement were difficult for the Puritans. About 400 people died during that time. But things started getting better, and more and more people moved to Massachusetts to join them. Ten years after the Puritans first landed, nearly 20,000 people lived in the colony. In time, the original settlement became several towns, including Newtown (now known as Cambridge), Lexington, Concord, Watertown, Charlestown, and many others.

As time went on, the settlers in the Massachusetts Bay Colony wanted more control over their own lives and less interference from England. King Charles II didn't want the colonists to be completely free to govern themselves, so in 1684 he canceled the Massachusetts Bay Company's charter. In 1691 England's King William III issued a new charter that unified the Massachusetts Bay Colony with the Plymouth Colony and other territories. The English government controlled the new colony, which was called the Province of Massachusetts Bay.

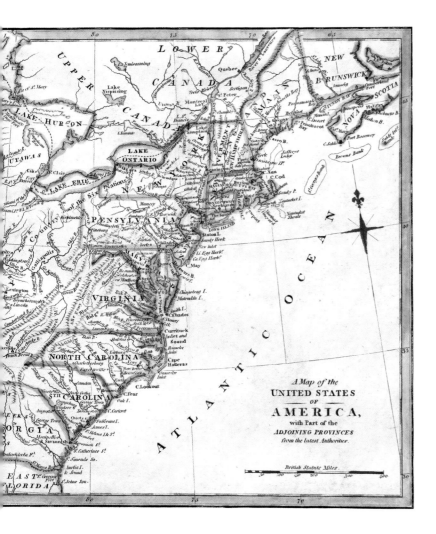

A Map of the
UNITED STATES
OF
AMERICA,
with Part of the
ADJOINING PROVINCES
from the latest Authorities.

British Statute Miles

HISTORY MAKERS

John Wheelwright (1592–1679) was the brother-in-law of Anne Hutchinson, who was banished from the Massachusetts Bay Colony because she wanted people to be able to worship God the way they wanted. Wheelwright was also banished from Massachusetts because he spoke out to defend his sister-in-law. After he founded the Exeter settlement, the settlers there signed the Exeter Compact, which was a lot like the Mayflower Compact.

INTERESTING!

Maryland got its name when King Charles I of England instructed Lord Baltimore to name the colony after Queen Henrietta Maria (Queen Mary), King Charles's wife.

Two Down, 11 to Go!

Over the next 112 years after the founding of the Massachusetts Colony, 11 more colonies that would one day become states were founded. Here is a quick look at those 11 colonies:

New Hampshire: In 1623 a group of English settlers arrived in northern New England and started a fishing village near the mouth of the Piscataqua River. In 1638 a settler named John Wheelwright, who had been banished from the Massachusetts Bay Colony because he didn't want to follow their laws and rules, founded a settlement in New Hampshire called Exeter. Massachusetts controlled this new colony until it became a colony of England in 1679.

Maryland: In 1632 King Charles I of England gave Lord Baltimore (his real name was George Calvert) land where Catholics could live and worship as they wanted. Lord Baltimore put his son, Cecil Calvert, in charge of starting settlements in the new colony. In 1633 the first settlers left England and sailed to what became the Maryland Colony.

Connecticut: In the mid-1630s, colonists began moving to the Colony of Connecticut, established by Thomas Hooker, who had left the Massachusetts Bay Colony because he didn't like the strict rules there. In 1639 three settlements united to form a government in Connecticut. They also created a document called the Fundamental Orders of Connecticut, the first written constitution (or set of rules to live by) in American history. Many historians believe the Fundamental Orders became the basis of the United States Constitution. In 1662 King Charles II of England officially united Connecticut as a single colony.

Rhode Island: The Puritan leaders in the Massachusetts Bay Colony were very strict with the colonists who lived there. The people were required to worship God in the way these leaders thought was right. A young minister named Roger Williams (about 1603–about 1683) disagreed with the strict rules and spoke out against them. In 1636, a year after the Puritans forced Williams to leave the Massachusetts Bay Colony, he started a new settlement near modern-day Providence, Rhode Island. Two years later, Anne Hutchinson, who had also been expelled from Massachusetts, helped form a colony at Portsmouth. Later, the Rhode Island colony was formed from these and two other settlements.

Delaware: In 1631 Dutch traders attempted to settle in a coastal area east of Maryland, but they were killed in fights with the local natives. In 1638 a man named Peter Minuit led a group of Swedish settlers to the Delaware River area. They named the settlement New Sweden. In 1655 Holland captured the land from the Swedish, but in 1664 the British defeated the Dutch and took control of the area. Delaware was part of Pennsylvania from 1682 until 1701. The people of Delaware elected a state assembly in 1704.

North Carolina and South Carolina: In 1653, a group of Virginia colonists traveled south and settled in a new area. Ten years later, King Charles II of England gave eight men permission to settle the area south of Virginia. These men created Carolina, which included the area settled in 1653. But in 1729, due to arguments among the people settled in the area, England took over the colony and split it into North Carolina and South Carolina.

New Jersey: Not long after Henry Hudson explored the mid-Atlantic coastline of North America, Dutch and Swedish settlers started arriving there. The Dutch named their part of the territory New Netherland, and the Swedish named their part New Sweden. In 1664 the Dutch and Swedes surrendered control of the area to England. That same year, King Charles II of England granted control of the area to his brother James, the Duke of York. James gave land to two of his friends, Lord Berkeley and Sir George Carteret, and they founded a colony that, in 1702, became the New Jersey Colony.

New York: In 1664 Charles II granted the Dutch colony of New Netherland to his brother, the Duke of York. All the duke had to do was take control away from the Dutch. When the British fleet arrived, the Dutch colonists surrendered without a fight. The British renamed the area (as well as the city of New Amsterdam) New York in honor of the Duke of York.

Pennsylvania: This colony was named after its founder, William Penn, the leader of a group of Christians called the Religious Society of Friends, or Quakers. The Quakers, like the Puritans, had been persecuted by the English, and many of them wanted to start a colony in America. Penn, who was the son of a British Navy admiral, founded the colony in 1682, and it quickly grew into one of the largest British colonies in the New World.

Georgia: Fifty years after the founding of the Pennsylvania Colony, the last of the 13 British colonies was formed. In 1732 a British general and member of Parliament named James Oglethorpe received permission from King George II to create a new settlement between South Carolina and Florida. In 1733 Oglethorpe led a group of settlers in founding the city of Savannah in the colony he named in honor of the king. Georgia became a British colony in 1752.

Spiritual Revival in the Colonies

In the 1730s and 1740s, the powerful preaching of men such as Jonathan Edwards, George Whitefield, and many others led to a revival in the colonies. This revival—in which many people became interested in spiritual things—became known as the First Great Awakening. (There were three "great awakenings" in US history.)

The First Great Awakening started with the preaching of Edwards, who was a minister in Northampton, Massachusetts, and one of the best-known preachers of the time. Edwards preached about sin and the need for salvation through Jesus Christ. A lot of colonists came to hear Edwards preach, and many of them became Christians as a result.

Other preachers began to copy Edwards's style, and some traveled around the colonies to preach. It wasn't long before the Great Awakening affected people all the way from northern New England down to Georgia. People from all walks of life—rich and poor, educated and uneducated, free and slave—either converted to Christianity or began to take their faith more seriously.

In 1739 and 1740, George Whitefield, a young British preacher, traveled to North America and began touring the colonies, preaching and

HISTORY MAKERS

Jonathan Edwards (1703–1758) was an American preacher and Bible expert who also worked as a missionary to Native Americans. His preaching led to a spiritual awakening in the colonies. His most famous sermon was titled "Sinners in the Hands of an Angry God." Edwards was born in East Windsor, Connecticut. He entered Yale University in the fall of 1716, a month before his thirteenth birthday, and graduated in 1720 as the top student in his class.

teaching. Whitefield's preaching style was very different from Jonathan Edwards's. While Edwards spoke slowly and in a serious tone, Whitefield spoke with more emotion and outward enthusiasm. His preaching attracted huge crowds everywhere he went, and countless people were converted to the Christian faith because of it.

The First Great Awakening was an important event in the history of the colonies that became the United States of America. It changed the way a lot of churches worshipped God, and it also brought Christianity to the African American slaves living and working in the colonies. It also led to what is called the evangelical movement, which emphasized the importance of spreading the message of the Gospel of Jesus Christ to people who hadn't heard it or didn't yet understand it.

Life in the Colonies

After reading about the founding of the 13 colonies, you might be wondering what life was like for the colonists. Well, a lot of that depended on which colony they lived in. The 13 colonies were established up and down the east coast of North America, and each colony had its own churches, local government, and ways of making a living.

Many historians divide the colonies into three geographical areas: the New England colonies (New Hampshire, Massachusetts, Rhode Island, and Connecticut), the middle colonies (New York, New Jersey, Pennsylvania, and Delaware), and the southern colonies (Maryland, Virginia, North Carolina, South Carolina, and Georgia).

The New England colonies were located in the North, where there were lots of forests as well as animals whose skins were valuable for trade. There were also a lot of rivers and harbors in the region, making it easier to ship goods to and from other countries and other colonies. Many New England colonists made their living by fishing, shipbuilding, harvesting trees for lumber, and fur trading. (The colonists often traded for furs with the Native Americans and shipped them overseas.) The soil in much of New England is rocky and therefore not very good for farming. For the most part, the farms in that area were big enough to provide for individual families, but too small to raise enough grain, vegetables, and fruit to trade with others.

The middle colonies enjoyed a good climate as well as good soil, and that allowed the colonists to make a living by farming. The farmers in the middle colonies planted and harvested grain and raised livestock for meat. The people of the middle colonies were known for making bread out of the grain the farmers harvested. There was a wide variety of jobs in the middle colonies.

People farmed or worked as tailors, glassblowers, silversmiths, and masons (stone and brick layers).

Of the three regions of colonies, the South was by far the best for farming. Those colonies were located on rich farmland that enjoyed excellent weather and long growing seasons. The people of the southern colonies grew most of their own food and also produced major cash crops such as tobacco, rice, and indigo (a plant that makes a bluish-purple dye)—none of which could be grown very well (if at all) in England. That is why the southern colonies did so much business with England. Most of these crops were grown on large farms called plantations, and the farmers usually used slaves to do the work. (You'll read more about slavery and how it divided the nation in Chapters 4 and 5).

Even though different colonies faced their own problems as they grew in size, one thing was true for all 13: Life was hard! The towns and villages weren't as well established as the ones in England that the people had come from; and just making it day to day was often a life-and-death struggle against the weather, disease, and hostile Native Americans.

But England was about to make things even worse for many of the colonists.

A Changing Relationship between England and Its Colonies

For the most part, the residents of the 13 colonies saw themselves as loyal subjects of the English king. But that was about to change, due mostly to the effects of the French and Indian War. Here's what happened:

During colonial times, England's main military rival was France. Eventually, England and France argued about ownership of the Ohio Territory and parts of Canada. When the dispute could not be settled by diplomacy (talks between national leaders), it was only a matter of time until war broke out between the British and the French.

It looked like the English would quickly and easily defeat the French. After all, they had a better-trained and better-equipped military. They also had the colonies, each of which had its own group of citizens who served in the army, known as the militia. However, the French had built a series of forts west of the Appalachian Mountains. One of those forts, Fort Duquesne, was located where Pittsburgh, Pennsylvania, is today.

In 1754 Lieutenant Colonel George Washington of the Virginia militia led a force of 150 soldiers in an effort to capture Fort Duquesne. Washington's men were badly outnumbered and were soon defeated by the French soldiers.

INTERESTING!

The Liberty Bell, which was made in 1752 and is now on display at Independence Hall in Philadelphia, has long been a symbol of American independence. The bell was inscribed with part of a Bible verse from Leviticus 25:10: "Proclaim liberty throughout all the land unto all the inhabitants thereof." The Liberty Bell was originally used to call lawmakers to legislative sessions and to let citizens know about public meetings and proclamations.

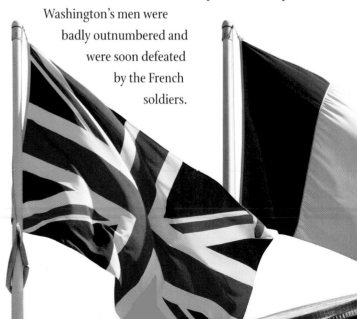

Later, Washington was captured, but he was allowed to return to Virginia with a message telling the British that the Ohio Territory belonged to the French.

In early July 1755, the British sent General Edward Braddock, their commander-in-chief for North America, along with George Washington and many soldiers, to attack Fort Duquesne. But the French, along with their Native American allies, won in a rout and General Braddock was killed in the battle. The French won because they fired from behind rocks and trees and other cover while the English troops marched in a straight line.

After the disastrous attack on Fort Duquesne, the British changed their strategy. They decided to fight the French in Canada instead. In 1763 after several years of fierce fighting in several big battles, Britain and France signed the Treaty of Paris, which stipulated that France would give up all claims to Canadian territories and the territory west of the colonies as far as the Mississippi River.

Who's Going to Pay for This War?

When the French and Indian War ended with England victorious, it was a relief to many people living in the 13 colonies. Great Britain's victory meant the British could keep Canada and several other territories in North America, and it also meant that the colonists didn't have to worry anymore about being taken over by the French.

But the colonists soon had another problem: To pay for the war effort, the British had gone into overwhelming debt. And because the war had been fought mostly to protect the American colonies, the British decided it was only right for the colonists, whom they still saw as their loyal subjects, to pay off that debt.

To help pay off its debt from the French and Indian War, the British government imposed sometimes steep taxes on the American colonies—and always without approval from the colonists.

Great Britain took in a lot of tax money from the colonists, who grew angrier and angrier because they were being taxed so heavily but couldn't do anything about it because they weren't represented in the British

HISTORY MAKERS

James Otis Jr. (1725–1783) was a lawyer in colonial Massachusetts and a member of the Massachusetts Legislature. Otis strongly supported the political views that eventually led to the American Revolution. Even though others had used the phrase "taxation without representation" before Otis, he is remembered for saying, "Taxation without representation is tyranny." Tyranny is the mean and unfair treatment of a weaker person or country by a stronger one.

Parliament, which made the laws in England. They said it was "taxation without representation."

Here are some of those taxes (and other laws imposed by England) and how they affected the colonists:

HISTORY MAKERS

John Dickinson (1732–1808), a politician from Pennsylvania, became known as the "Penman of the Revolution" after his pamphlet *Letters from a Farmer in Pennsylvania*, which protested the Quartering Act, was printed and distributed throughout the colonies. Here are some words from that pamphlet:

If the British Parliament has a legal authority to issue an order that we shall furnish a single article for the troops here and compel obedience to that order, they have the same right to issue an order for us to supply those troops with arms, clothes, and every necessary, and to compel obedience to that order also; in short, to lay any burdens they please upon us. What is this but taxing us at a certain sum and leaving to us only the manner of raising it? How is this mode more tolerable than the Stamp Act?

Sugar Act:

This 1764 law imposed a three-cent tax on foreign refined sugar and also increased taxes on coffee, indigo, and certain kinds of wine. It also banned the importation of rum and French wines into the colonies. These taxes didn't affect the general population in the colonies, but they were imposed without the colonists' consent.

Stamp Act:

This was the first direct British tax on American colonists. Imposed in November 1765, it required every newspaper, pamphlet, and other public and legal document to carry a British seal or stamp, which cost money. The colonists protested the tax, and the British government repealed (or canceled) it in 1766. At the time of the repeal, though, the British passed another law, the Declaratory Act, which said that Great Britain was superior to, and held rule over, the American colonies.

Quartering Act: In March 1765, the British Parliament passed a law to address the needs of British soldiers who had been sent to the colonies to keep the peace. The law required each colonial assembly to provide British soldiers housing (or "quarters"), bedding, and other necessities of life. Parliament expanded this to require the colonies to house soldiers in taverns and unoccupied houses. The colonists opposed this act because they were afraid of having the British army in all their towns and villages, and because they were having to pay to care for the British soldiers. Even though it wasn't a direct tax on the colonists, the Quartering Act cost the colonists a lot of money.

Townshend Acts: This was a series of 1767 laws, named for Charles Townshend, the British treasurer, that imposed new taxes on glass, lead, paints, paper, and tea. The colonists reacted to these new taxes the same way they did to the Sugar Act and Stamp Act. Eventually Britain repealed all the taxes except the tax on tea.

The British Parliament's new laws and new taxes on the 13 colonies served only to anger and frustrate the colonists as time went on. The final straw came on May 10, 1773, when Parliament passed the Tea Act. Even

HISTORIC HAPPENINGS

On March 5, 1770, five civilians died and several others were wounded when British soldiers opened fire on a gathering in Boston, Massachusetts. Both sides disputed the cause of the shootings, which came to be known as the Boston Massacre, but the violence helped spark a rebellion in some of the colonies and eventually led to the Revolutionary War.

though the Tea Act didn't impose any new taxes on the colonists, it hurt colonial businessmen because it meant that more British tea would be shipped to the colonies and sold at lower prices.

The colonists had agreed not to buy things they had previously bought from English traders (an act called a boycott), including clothes, paper, and tea. But on December 16, 1773, a group of colonists, some dressed up as Native Americans, showed the British how serious they were about taxation without representation (and how much they disliked the Tea Act) when they boarded three English ships docked in Boston Harbor and threw their cargo of tea overboard.

This incident is known today as the Boston Tea Party, and it led to a series of new British laws that moved the colonists and the British military closer to war. ✖

CHAPTER 3

The Birth of the United States

The Revolutionary War through George Washington's Presidency

After the French and Indian War, the relationship between the 13 colonies and England began a fast downward spiral, as England continued to impose laws and levy taxes on the colonists without allowing them to be represented in Parliament.

The tension finally reached a boiling point after the Boston Tea Party. As one incident followed another, it began to appear that it was only a matter of time before military conflict broke out in North America.

In this chapter, you'll read about the last few events that led to the Revolutionary War—also known as the War for Independence. You'll also read about how the colonists won their independence in a David-and-Goliath-type war against a better-armed, more experienced British military. And you'll also read about how the newly formed United States, after some struggles, finally established its own government.

We're Not Gonna Take It Anymore!

The British government responded to the Boston Tea Party by passing several new laws meant to punish the colonists. One of those laws completely shut down Boston Harbor until the colonists had paid for the tea they had dumped into the water. Some of the new laws took away the colonists' freedom and required that they get permission from the British government before they held any public meetings. The British government also greatly limited the power of the individual colonies' legislatures (the groups that make laws).

The colonists referred to these new laws as "intolerable acts," and they became convinced they needed to take strong steps to protect themselves and their freedoms. To do that, 56 delegates representing the 13 colonies gathered in Philadelphia on September 5, 1774, for a meeting of the First Continental Congress. For the first time, the 13 colonies worked together to protect their individual freedoms and liberties.

HISTORY MAKERS

In 1750 a Virginia physician and explorer named Thomas Walker discovered the Cumberland Gap, a pass through the Appalachian Mountains long used by Native Americans. In 1775 as war between the colonies and England grew near, a Pennsylvanian-born frontiersman named Daniel Boone (1734–1820) was busy blazing his Wilderness Road along a trail through the Cumberland Gap. Boone and a team of 35 axmen widened the trail, making it possible for later pioneers to journey through the Appalachians from Virginia to Kentucky and Tennessee.

The First Continental Congress didn't waste much time before declaring at least some independence from England. It passed a resolution limiting the power of the British Parliament, including a declaration that Parliament would no longer be allowed to pass laws for the colonies. Parliament's right, as far as the colonies were concerned, would be only to regulate trade between the colonies and England. Finally, the Congress resolved that by December 1774, the colonies would no longer buy anything from Great Britain; and by September 1775, they would stop shipping goods to England.

Getting Ready for War

Many, if not most, of the colonists suffered because of what was happening between the 13 colonies and Great Britain, but the people in Boston had it far worse than others. After the English navy closed Boston Harbor, Boston merchants could no longer trade with other nations. Many colonists in Boston lost their jobs. Even worse, Great Britain sent huge numbers of soldiers to Boston, and the people there were expected to feed and house them.

By April 1775, tensions between the British and the colonists were very high, and some of the 13 colonies had already begun assembling volunteer armies to defend themselves if the British attacked.

Meanwhile, Great Britain ordered the Massachusetts governor to send troops to Boston to take away all the people's weapons and ammunition. Since the British military was the best trained and strongest in the world at that time, they expected little resistance when they marched into Boston.

What the British didn't know, however, was that the colonists were ready to fight. They had gathered a group of volunteer soldiers, called "minutemen" for their ability to assemble on a minute's notice. These farmers, shopkeepers, and common workers would immediately respond to any threat from the British.

The Battles of Lexington and Concord

On the night of April 18, 1775, about 700 British soldiers (also called Redcoats for the color of their uniforms), under the command of Lieutenant Colonel Francis Smith, marched from Boston toward Concord, where the colonists had hidden weapons and ammunition.

There were two things Smith and his men didn't know: First, weeks before the march, the militiamen had learned of the plan to capture their supplies and had moved them to other hiding places. Second, the militiamen knew about the planned attack, and they were able to mobilize quickly as the British troops drew near Concord.

Late that night, a silversmith named Paul Revere, and several other men on horseback, spotted the British soldiers as they marched toward Concord. The men rode out ahead of the advancing army to warn the militias, shouting, "The Redcoats are coming! The Redcoats are coming!" The warning gave the minutemen all the time they needed to prepare to stand up to the British soldiers.

The first shots of the Revolutionary War were fired near Lexington, Massachusetts, at sunrise on the morning of April 19, 1775. The

INTERESTING!

Even though Paul Revere became the most famous of the men who rode their horses through the countryside warning the colonists that the British were on their way, he actually never made it to Concord. Instead, he was captured by the Redcoats, who released him after he gave them a lot of false or misleading information. One of Revere's companions, a man named Samuel Prescott, avoided capture and got the message through to Concord. When the British arrived, the colonists were ready.

HISTORIC HAPPENINGS

Sometimes historians can point to a single moment as the start of an armed conflict. The American Revolution is an example. At dawn on April 19, 1775, in Lexington, Massachusetts, 77 minutemen stood face-to-face with more than 700 Redcoats. Just then, someone's musket—no one knows for sure whose it was—went off. Within seconds, eight colonists were dead and nine wounded. The rest retreated, joined up with other militiamen, and chased the British toward Concord, where the battle continued. Just like that, the Revolutionary War had begun!

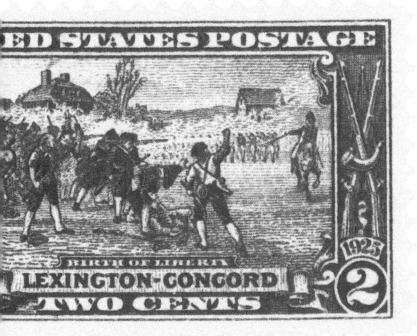

ED STATES POSTAGE

BIRTH OF LIBERTY

LEXINGTON-CONCORD

TWO CENTS

1925

2

In January 1776, a writer named Thomas Paine wrote a pamphlet he titled *Common Sense*, which outlined the reasons it was time for the colonies to declare their independence from Great Britain and form their own nation. Many colonists read Paine's pamphlet, and thousands came to the same conclusion: It was time to break away from Great Britain. The pamphlet also changed the opinions of some colonial leaders who believed it was still possible for the colonies to settle their differences with Great Britain without going to war.

minutemen were heavily outnumbered and had to retreat at first, and the British troops continued their march toward Concord.

At the North Bridge in Concord, 500 minutemen attacked and defeated the British soldiers. Historians say this could have turned into a massacre had reinforcements not arrived as the British retreated and began heading back toward Lexington. About 1,700 British soldiers now began their march back to Boston, but they came under heavy fire from the militias. Eventually, the British troops made it to safety in Charlestown, Massachusetts.

Meanwhile, the militiamen surrounded Boston, preventing the British army from moving in and out of the city. After an 11-month period, called the Siege of Boston, the British were forced to withdraw from the town completely.

For the British, who believed their military was the finest in the world, the defeats in the battles of Lexington and Concord, as well as their retreat from Boston following the Siege of Boston, were embarrassing and humiliating. For the colonists, though, they were encouraging signs that they could stand up to the greatest military force in the world and come out victorious.

Extending an Olive Branch

Even though shots had been exchanged between the colonists and the British troops, and even though people on both sides had been wounded or killed, the two sides had not yet engaged in all-out war. In an effort to avoid war—and to prepare for it, if it was unavoidable—the Second Continental Congress began meeting in May 1775.

The Congress formed the American Continental Army, which coordinated the efforts of the militias of the 13 colonies. It also took additional steps to move the colonies toward independence from Great Britain. Though it had no formal authority, the Continental Congress

acted as the national government of what would become the United States of America.

Some of the more radical members of the Second Continental Congress, led by John Adams, a representative from Massachusetts, believed it wasn't possible to avoid a full-blown war. But in July 1775, the Congress passed a resolution, written by John Dickinson of Pennsylvania and known as the Olive Branch Petition, which stated that the colonies did not want to go to war and were not seeking to become independent. They sent a written copy to King George III.

King George refused to even read the petition. Instead, he declared that the colonies had engaged in open rebellion against the king and against Great Britain.

King George III's refusal to even read the Olive Branch Petition pushed the colonies toward a choice between two options: They could either surrender unconditionally and remain subjects of Great Britain, or they could go to war to win their independence. Samuel Adams, a member of the Continental Congress, believed that King George had given the colonies an opportunity to make their push for independence from England.

There was still an opportunity for the colonies to avoid all-out war with Great Britain, but that opportunity ended in the summer of 1776, when the Continental Congress established a new nation called the United States of America.

WORTH REPEATING

"Believe me, dear sir: there is not in the British Empire a man who more cordially loves a union with Great Britain than I do. But, by the God that made me, I will cease to exist before I yield to a connection such terms as the British Parliament propose; and in this, I think I speak the sentiments of America."
—Thomas Jefferson, November 29, 1775

INTERESTING!

Although the Second Continental Congress approved the final wording of the Declaration of Independence on July 4, 1776, the actual date of its signing by the delegates from the 13 colonies isn't certain. Most historians believe the delegates signed it on August 2, 1776, a month after it was adopted.

The Declaration of Independence

Have you ever thought about what the July 4 holiday we celebrate every summer really means? If you're like a lot of Americans, you know it's a time when families and friends get together for picnics during the day and flashy, noisy fireworks displays after dark.

You probably know that the real name of the holiday is Independence Day. This is the day we celebrate and remember what some very courageous and motivated Americans did on July 4, 1776. On that day, the Second Continental Congress formally adopted the Declaration of Independence, which was a letter to King George III of England stating that the 13 colonies would no longer be part of the British Empire and also explaining why they had declared their independence.

The Continental Congress gave a highly educated Virginian named Thomas Jefferson the responsibility of writing a declaration of independence that would be sent to Great Britain once it was finished. After Jefferson finished writing the declaration, and after the Continental Congress officially approved it, a new, independent nation was born.

What's Really in the Declaration of Independence?

The Declaration of Independence begins by stating that sometimes it becomes necessary for one group of people to break away from another—in this case, the colonies broke away from Great Britain—to form their own nation, which is in keeping with the laws and the nature of God. It then explains that it is necessary to explain why they are splitting off to become an independent nation.

The declaration includes one of the best-known statements about human freedom of any document in history: "We hold these truths to be self-evident, that all men are created equal, that they are endowed by their Creator with certain unalienable rights, that among these are life, liberty, and the pursuit of happiness." The declaration says that when any human government gets in the way of those God-given rights, the people have the right to either make changes in the government or get rid of it completely.

INTERESTING!

Most of the Founding Fathers of the United States were Christian men who believed the Bible. Almost half of the 56 men who signed the Declaration of Independence—24 to be exact—had earned degrees in Bible school or seminary.

The declaration presents a long list of the 13 colonies' complaints against King George III. Here are some highlights of that list, put in words that are easier to understand than the original:

The king won't allow us to pass laws that are for the good of everyone who lives here.

Even when the king allows us to pass laws, he won't allow us to put them into effect.

The king forces us to give up our rights to make the laws we need.

The king calls lawmakers to meet at the most inconvenient times, and in distant places, so that they can't show up to pass the laws.

The king takes away our rights by dissolving our representative bodies.

The king won't allow us to elect new representatives.

The king won't allow new settlers to come to America, or he puts difficult conditions on their immigration.

The king refuses to allow us to appoint our own judges, but instead appoints judges who always agree with him.

A total of 56 men signed the Declaration of Independence. These men, along with others who took part in the Revolutionary War or the drafting of the United States Constitution, are called the Founding Fathers of the United States of America. The most famous of those signatures was that of John Hancock, the president of the Continental Congress, because he was the first man to sign and he signed his name so big. Among the signers were two future presidents of the United States: John Adams (second president) and Thomas Jefferson (third president). Here is the complete list of the signers, by their home states:

Delaware: George Read, Caesar Rodney, Thomas McKean

Pennsylvania: George Clymer, Robert Morris, Benjamin Rush, James Smith, George Taylor, Benjamin Franklin, John Morton, George Ross, James Wilson

Massachusetts: John Adams, John Hancock, Elbridge Gerry, Samuel Adams, Robert Treat Paine

New Hampshire: Josiah Bartlett, William Whipple, Matthew Thornton

Rhode Island: Stephen Hopkins, William Ellery

New York: Lewis Morris, Francis Lewis, Philip Livingston, William Floyd

Georgia: Button Gwinnett, Lyman Hall, George Walton

Virginia: Richard Henry Lee, Carter Braxton, Thomas Jefferson, Thomas Nelson Jr., Francis Lightfoot Lee, Benjamin Harrison, George Wythe

North Carolina: William Hooper, John Penn, Joseph Hewes

South Carolina: Edward Rutledge, Arthur Middleton, Thomas Lynch Jr., Thomas Heyward Jr.

New Jersey: Abraham Clark, Francis Hopkinson, John Witherspoon, John Hart, Richard Stockton

Connecticut: Samuel Huntington, William Williams, Roger Sherman, Oliver Wolcott

Maryland: Charles Carroll, Thomas Stone, Samuel Chase, William Paca

The king sends us new government officials we don't want, and he makes us pay them.

Even in times of peace, the king sends British soldiers here without our permission, and those soldiers don't even have to obey our laws.

The king forces us to buy goods from England, even goods we can buy somewhere else.

The king imposes taxes on us without giving us any choice.

The king won't allow us to try accused criminals by jury, but instead sends people accused of pretend crimes back to England for their trials.

The king does everything he can to destroy our lives, including burning down our towns.

The king sends foreign soldiers to bring death, destruction, and tyranny.

The king takes our fellow Americans against their will and forces them to fight against their own friends and family.

The king tries to get our own people to revolt against our government and tries to get Native Americans to attack us.

When we complain about how the king has treated us, he only treats us worse.

The Declaration of Independence concludes by stating that the United States would be a new and independent nation made up of free and independent states that would no longer be under the authority of the British crown and that they would have the power and authority to wage war, to make alliances and treaties with other nations, to trade with any nation they wanted to, and do everything else an independent nation has the right to do.

You can read the original words of the Declaration of Independence in Appendix B (page 149).

Copies of this new document called the Declaration of Independence were soon distributed throughout the colonies, which served to make the people more determined to break free of British rule.

The signers of the declaration knew the terrible, personal risks they took by signing the document. They also knew the declaration ensured that there would be no peaceful solution to the differences between the colonies and King George III.

A Revolutionary War

When King George III learned that the colonies had declared their independence from Great Britain, he sent many more soldiers to the colonies to fight. The colonists didn't look like much of a match for the British, who had the most powerful military force in the world at that time.

The colonial forces had become more organized by then, however. On June 14, 1775, the Continental Congress established the Continental Army to help coordinate the efforts of the 13 colonies in their rebellion against the rule of Great Britain. The Continental Congress appointed General George Washington as commander of the Continental Army.

The war was very hard on all the colonies, and many times it looked as if the British were going to win. But under Washington's courageous leadership, the American soldiers fought on.

Even though the Continental Army was fighting a powerful enemy, it had one key advantage. The colonial soldiers were defending their own homeland, while most of the British soldiers had been shipped over from England. Though the British at first had superior military forces, the Americans began winning important battles as the war went on.

WORTH REPEATING

"Resistance to tyranny becomes the Christian and social duty of each individual. . . . Continue steadfast and, with a proper sense of your dependence on God, nobly defend those rights which heaven gave, and no man ought to take from us."
—John Hancock, first signer of the Declaration of Independence

King George III

Help...from Great Britain's European Neighbors

Early on in the war, France, Spain, and the Dutch Republic (now known as the Netherlands) sent supplies, weapons, and ammunition to the colonies, but none of them wanted to get involved directly in the war.

HISTORY MAKERS

Benjamin Franklin (1706–1790) was one of the Founding Fathers of the United States and a great statesman and diplomat. He was also a writer, scientist, and inventor. Franklin invented the lightning rod, bifocals, the Franklin stove, an odometer for horse-drawn carriages, and a musical instrument called a "glass armonica." Franklin made many discoveries about electricity and also formed America's first public lending library and a fire department in Pennsylvania. After his death on April 17, 1790, approximately 20,000 people attended his funeral.

After some early British success, the war became a standoff, meaning neither side was winning or losing. The British navy was far superior to anything the colonists could muster, so the British controlled the American coastline. The American patriots, on the other hand, controlled the countryside, where 90 percent of the population lived.

In 1778 France became an ally of the Americans. Most historians agree this key development was necessary if the colonies were to win their independence.

Not long after the Continental Congress adopted the Declaration of Independence, they appointed Benjamin Franklin as minister to France. Franklin asked the French for help in the war, but at first they were reluctant to enter into another war with England. Eventually however, Franklin persuaded the French to openly enter the war (it also didn't hurt that the French saw that the colonies were having success in the war), and on February 6, 1778, the Treaty of Alliance with France was signed. As part of the treaty, France provided transportation to America for French officers, soldiers, and weapons.

Over the next two years, Spain and the Dutch Republic also went to war with Great Britain. Even in England, many Britons sided with the Americans.

With all that help, especially from French general Lafayette and other French soldiers, the United States won several big battles against the British. Finally in August 1788, after a French naval victory over the British in Chesapeake Bay, the English formally surrendered to George Washington at Yorktown, Pennsylvania.

Key Battles in the Revolutionary War

Earlier, you read how the battles of Lexington and Concord marked the beginning of the Revolutionary War. Here are some other important battles in that war:

The Battle of Bunker Hill (June 17, 1775): Just

days after the Continental Congress named General George Washington commander-in-chief of the Continental Army, the British started this battle (which was actually fought at Breed's Hill) when British general William Howe led 2,600 soldiers up into battle in Boston. British warships also fired on the patriots. The Americans fought bravely but had to retreat after a third charge by the British. Though the Americans withdrew, the Redcoats suffered heavy losses in this battle.

The Battle of Long Island (August 27, 1776): This

was the first major battle following the Declaration of Independence. The British had just lost Boston, so they were determined to take control of New York City, which they knew was important to the colonies because it was a key point of communication between the North and the South. In April 1776, General Washington, anticipating the arrival of the British, began positioning about 20,000 troops at the western end of Long Island. The British fleet arrived with 45,000 troops, and when they attacked, Washington was forced to cross the East River into Manhattan. After several more battles, the British drove the Continental Army completely out of New York City.

The Battle of Trenton (December 25, 1776):

After being forced to retreat from New York, General Washington knew his troops needed a victory to boost their morale. So on a snowy, icy evening on Christmas 1776, he led 2,500 soldiers across the Delaware River to Trenton, New Jersey, where the Americans attacked a group of British soldiers. The Americans caught the British soldiers completely by

HISTORIC HAPPENINGS

If you've ever wondered how much difficulty the soldiers from the Continental Army faced as they fought to win freedom for America—including *your* freedom—consider what some of them endured during the winter of 1777-1778. During a cold, snowy Pennsylvania winter, General George Washington's men camped at Valley Forge, living in tents until they were able to build some huts for shelter. Though they struggled just to survive—most of the men did not have warm clothing or adequate shoes—they emerged a stronger army as a result. Throughout the winter, they worked to improve their fighting skills. When spring finally came, they were more experienced and more disciplined, and ready to take on the British army.

surprise—most of them were sleeping—and killed more than 100 men and took 1,000 prisoners. Not a single American was killed, and the victory gave the Americans a big boost in morale.

The Battle of Princeton (January 3, 1777): Fresh off their victory at Trenton, General Washington's troops defeated the British at the Battle of Princeton.

The Battles of Saratoga (September 19 and October 7, 1777): This was a major victory for the American forces and a turning point in the Revolutionary War. The Americans fought British general John Burgoyne's army at Saratoga, New York. By the time the battles were over, the Americans had killed 440 British soldiers, wounded 695 more, and taken 6,222 captive. News of this American victory encouraged France to join the colonists against the British.

The Battle of Yorktown (September 28 to October 19, 1781): This battle didn't officially end the Revolutionary War, but it was the last major skirmish. General George Washington and French general Jean-Baptiste Ponton de Rochambeau led a combined force of American and French soldiers into battle against the forces of British lieutenant general Charles Cornwallis in the battle at Yorktown, Virginia. The combined French and American forces routed the British, and the battle ended when Cornwallis surrendered on October 19, 1781. This was the beginning of the end of the Revolutionary War.

Peace Breaks Out in America

On September 3, 1783, the Treaty of Paris was signed, officially ending the war. The Treaty of Paris recognized the United States as an independent nation and granted it control of the territories bounded on the east by the Atlantic Ocean, on the north by what is now Canada, on the south by Florida, and on the west by the Mississippi River.

The Americans had fought bravely—against their British enemies as well as against sometimes terrible weather—and had come out victorious against a military force that by all rights should have defeated them easily. But win they did, and now it was time to get down to the business of forming a government and beginning life as a new nation—the United States of America.

The Articles of Confederation

As the Revolutionary War raged on, the Continental Congress wrote a document called the Articles of Confederation, which was intended to provide the colonies some sort of unified government. On March 1, 1781, about three years after the Americans won their independence from the British, the 13 colonies ratified the Articles of Confederation, meaning it was now the law of the land in the United States.

The Articles of Confederation made the states and their legislatures supreme and gave each state the right to pass and enforce its own laws and collect taxes. The central government of the United States, however, was very weak and had very little authority to oversee interactions between the states. There was no executive branch (meaning a president and a cabinet, like we have today) and only limited judicial functions. The federal (national) government had no authority to collect taxes of any kind, and as a result, the nation went into debt that it couldn't repay.

It wasn't long before the leaders of the United States realized that having such a weak central government was not good for the states or for the unity of the new nation. Efforts to strengthen the central government failed, so in May 1787, a convention of representatives, or delegates, from 12 of the 13 states (Rhode Island refused to send representatives because it didn't want to lose the rights it had as a state) gathered to draft an entirely new constitution.

The Constitutional Convention

More than 50 delegates from the 12 participating states met in Philadelphia in May 1787 to begin drafting a new constitution. This was a gathering of some of the best-educated and most experienced men in the United States. They ranged in age from 40 to 81 (Benjamin Franklin was the oldest). Some were

HOW OUR GOVERNMENT WORKS

When the Founding Fathers met in Philadelphia to draft the United States Constitution, they wanted to prevent any one person, or group of people, from having too much power. But they didn't want a weak federal government with no power at all, like it had been under the Articles of Confederation. To protect the rights and liberties of all American citizens, the new government was divided between three separate but equal branches: the executive branch (the president and his cabinet), the legislative branch (the Congress, which passes laws), and the judicial branch (the courts, which interpret and apply the laws that the Congress passes).

Here is a quick look at the three branches of the federal government and the roles they play:

The Executive Branch: The president of the United States is the head of this branch of government. The president's power to create laws is limited to providing leadership and developing policies. The president can suggest new laws, but can't pass them without the approval of Congress.

The Legislative Branch: Each state is represented in the legislative branch, also known as Congress, by two senators and a number of members of the House of Representatives, based on the population of the state. The Senate and the House work together to make the nation's laws, but they also give more balance to the federal government, because a bill must pass both houses of Congress before it can become law. Once Congress passes a bill, the president can either sign it into law or veto it—which means to keep it from becoming law.

The Judicial Branch: This branch of the federal government examines the laws Congress passes to see if they meet with the standards of the Constitution and to make sure they don't violate the rights of citizens. The judicial branch has several levels, and the United States Supreme Court has the final say about whether a law is constitutional.

wealthy landowners, while others were lawyers or judges. One thing they had in common was that they had held at least one public office.

As the convention began, the delegates discussed and debated the problems the Articles of Confederation had presented. But as the convention wore on, they decided that it made more sense to create a whole new constitution and a whole new central government than it did to rewrite the Articles of Confederation.

On September 17, 1787, after about four months of debate, arguing, and compromise, the delegates signed the Constitution of the United States, making it the law of the United States of America and creating a new federal government that had more power than the confederation of states that it replaced.

Our First President

WASHINGTON

The United States Constitution established that the new nation would be led by a president—one whose powers are limited by the balance among the three branches of government—and not by a monarch (a king or queen). It also held that the president would not be elected by a popular vote of the people but by the state legislatures, which were elected by the people. This type of government is called a republic.

At first, not everyone could vote for the electors like we can today. Only white men who owned property were allowed to vote. On January 7, 1789, American voters chose their first state electors, who cast their votes for the first president of the United States.

Most people expected that George Washington, who had become a national hero when he led the Continental Army so brilliantly during the Revolutionary War, would easily win the election, and that is exactly what happened. Washington won unanimously, taking every elector's vote, and was sworn into office on April 30, 1789. John Adams was elected the nation's first vice president.

Washington was again elected unanimously in 1792, and John Adams was again elected vice president. Washington would almost certainly have won a third term, but he refused to run because he believed no man should have that much power for that long.

George Washington's Legacy

By now you probably know that George Washington was the most important of the Founding Fathers. He led the Continental Army to victory over the British, played a key role in the forming of the US Constitution, and served two terms as president.

Washington's presidency was one of the most important in US history. In 1791, during his first term in office, 10 amendments—also known as the Bill of Rights—were made to the US Constitution.

About four years after the Constitution was signed into law, James Madison—a representative for the state of Virginia and later the fourth president of the United States—introduced 10 amendments to limit the power of the federal government and protect the freedom of individual American citizens from the government and from the whims of the majority.

The first United States Congress passed the Bill of Rights on September 25, 1789, and they officially became a part of the Constitution on December 15, 1791, after two-thirds of the states ratified (officially approved) them.

George Washington's cabinet (or group of close advisers) included Secretary of State Thomas Jefferson (who wrote the Declaration of Independence and eventually became the third president of the United States), Secretary of the Treasury Alexander Hamilton (who was instrumental in designing the United States Constitution), Secretary of War Henry Knox (a high-ranking officer during the Revolutionary War), and Attorney General Edmund Randolph (one of the 11 delegates from Virginia in the 1779 Continental Congress). Historians

INTERESTING!

A lot of things have changed since that first United States presidential election in 1789. For one thing, *all* American citizens age 18 and older have the right to vote in presidential elections. One thing that hasn't changed much is the process we use to elect our presidents. Presidential elections are still decided by what is called the Electoral College system, meaning that individual voters vote in their states for electors, who in turn vote for president.

WORTH REPEATING

"I walk on untrodden ground. There is scarcely any part of my conduct that may not hereafter be drawn into precedent."
—George Washington, after being elected to his first term as US president

INTERESTING!

Most people believe that George Washington wore false teeth made of wood. While it's true he had lost his natural teeth and had to wear false ones, his fake choppers weren't made of wood but of hippopotamus ivory and gold. They were made by Dr. John Greenwood, who came to be known as the "father of modern dentistry."

HISTORY MAKERS

Eli Whitney (1765–1825) was an American inventor who is best known for inventing the cotton gin, a mechanical device that removes seeds from cotton. Before Whitney invented the cotton gin in 1793, people had to remove cotton seeds by hand, which went very slowly. The cotton gin helped make cotton an important cash crop in the South, which in turn led to the growth of slavery in that part of the country. (By the way, the word *gin* is short for "engine.")

remember Washington as a president who relied heavily on his cabinet for advice in domestic and foreign affairs alike.

Washington stopped the first serious challenge to federal authority when he sent troops to suppress the Whiskey Rebellion of 1794, in which Pennsylvania farmers refused to pay a tax. (The Constitution says that the federal government has the right to collect taxes.)

When it came to relationships with other nations, Washington believed strongly in neutrality, meaning he believed the United States should not take sides and should stay out of other nations' wars. He was criticized when he declared the Proclamation of Neutrality in 1793 because many people believed he owed more support to France, which had been so helpful during the Revolutionary War. Washington restated his belief in neutrality during his Farewell Address in 1796, when he warned the United States against becoming involved in foreign conflicts. His words helped shape American foreign policy for many decades to come.

THE FIRST TEN AMENDMENTS TO THE US CONSTITUTION (THE BILL OF RIGHTS)

First Amendment—Guarantees freedom of religion, speech, and the press, as well as the right to assemble and petition (or make requests to) the government.
Second Amendment—Guarantees the right to keep and bear arms (guns).
Third Amendment—Prohibits the forced housing of soldiers during times of peace.
Fourth Amendment—Prohibits unreasonable searches and seizures and spells out requirements for search warrants.
Fifth Amendment—Lays out rules for how a person accused of a crime can be put on trial, protects people on trial from having to testify against themselves, and protects people from being put on trial twice for the same crime. Also, this amendment keeps the government from taking somebody's private property for public use without paying a fair price for it.
Sixth Amendment—Guarantees the right to a fair and speedy trial by jury, the right to confront your accuser, the right to have witnesses at your trial, and the right to have a lawyer help you at the trial.
Seventh Amendment—Guarantees the right to a trial by jury in certain noncriminal (civil) cases.
Eighth Amendment—Prohibits excessive fines, excessive bail, and cruel and unusual punishment.
Ninth Amendment—Protects rights and liberties not specifically mentioned in the Constitution.
Tenth Amendment—Limits the powers of the federal government to those given to it by the United States Constitution.

CHAPTER 4

A Young Nation's Growing Pains

The Westward Expansion of the United States

Before the Revolutionary War, not many colonists made their way west to explore and settle the land west of the Appalachian Mountains. That's mostly because the Appalachians were difficult to pass.

Three things changed that. First, Daniel Boone blazed his Wilderness Road through the Cumberland Gap, making it easier for explorers and settlers to negotiate the rugged Appalachian terrain. Second, Great Britain and the newly formed United States signed the 1783 Treaty of Paris, which ended the Revolutionary War and gave the United States all land east to the Mississippi River. Finally, in 1787, the Continental Congress passed the Northwest Ordinance, which encouraged Americans to settle in the Northwest Territory, which the United States acquired after winning the Revolutionary War and which included land that became the states of Ohio, Indiana, Illinois, Michigan, and Wisconsin.

With the war over, a new pass cleared over the mountains, and a lot of new land to explore and settle, it wasn't long before Americans began moving west to explore and settle previously unknown places. By 1810, an estimated 200,000 to 300,000 people had traveled the Wilderness Trail on their way to Kentucky and the Ohio Valley.

In this chapter, you'll learn about the westward expansion of the United States and about the difficulties these people, called *pioneers*, faced as they explored and settled in new territory. You will also learn about how the United States acquired territories in the West that later became US states.

America's Biggest Bargain: The Louisiana Purchase

By the turn of the nineteenth century (another way of saying the beginning of the 1800s), three more territories had joined the original 13 colonies as states: Vermont in 1791, Kentucky in 1792, and Tennessee in 1796. The population of the United States was growing very quickly, and many people began looking for still more land where they could raise their families and make a living.

The US government also wanted more land. Thomas Jefferson, the third president of the United States, knew that the Louisiana Territory, which France owned at the time, had a lot of land—as much as or more than the United States already had. It also included the Mississippi River and the city of New Orleans, an important port

city at the mouth of the Mississippi. Jefferson believed that making New Orleans part of the United States would make it easier to protect American shipping and settlements along the Mississippi.

Jefferson thought France might be willing to sell part of the Louisiana Territory. In 1802 he sent Robert Livingston, one of the Founding Fathers of the United States, to France with an offer to see if Emperor Napoleon Bonaparte would be willing to sell New Orleans and part of the banks of the Mississippi River. Livingston was authorized to offer $10 million for the land. At first, Napoleon refused the offer because he planned to expand his own empire into parts of North America. But Jefferson didn't want to give up on the idea, so he sent James Monroe, another Founding Father (who later became the fifth president of the United States), to France to see if Napoleon would reconsider America's offer.

Driving a Hard Bargain

The Americans had one big advantage in their goal of acquiring at least some of the Louisiana Territory: Napoleon was at war at the time, and it wasn't going well for him. He needed money to help his cause. Besides, he was so busy fighting his wars in Europe that it probably would have been impossible to pursue expansion in North America.

After Monroe traveled to France, Napoleon had a big change of heart. The French emperor offered to sell the United States *all* of the Louisiana Territory—828,000 square miles of land—and not just New Orleans and some of the banks of the Mississippi. Napoleon had just one condition for selling the Louisiana Territory to the Americans: They would have to kick in another $5 million.

The offer shocked both Livingston and Monroe. Even though they hadn't been authorized to spend $15 million, they accepted the offer before Napoleon had a chance to think it over. They obviously knew a great deal when they saw it! On April 30, 1803, the two Americans signed the Louisiana Purchase Treaty. After some debate, the US Congress ratified the treaty. The final transfer of funds to France came later that year, officially making the Louisiana Territory part of the United States.

WORTH REPEATING

"We have lived long, but this is the noblest work of our whole lives. . . . From this day the United States take their place among the powers of the first rank."
—Robert Livingston, after signing the Louisiana Purchase Treaty

The successful purchase of the Louisiana Territory was huge for America. Not only did it give the United States control of the Mississippi River—*all* of the Mississippi River!—and the port city of New Orleans, it also *doubled* the size of the United States. The purchase gave the United States territories that later became the states of Oklahoma, Nebraska, Kansas, Iowa, and Missouri, and parts of the land that became the states of Louisiana, Texas, Minnesota, Colorado, New Mexico, Wyoming, Montana, South Dakota, and North Dakota.

The Louisiana Purchase made it easier for American farmers to ship their crops to other countries and also peacefully eliminated a rival—France—that could have threatened the United States.

Checking Out the New Land

In the early 1800s, many people believed it was possible to cross the North American continent by sailing on a chain of rivers that stretched from the Mississippi River to the Pacific Ocean. If someone could find that chain, it would make travel from the eastern part of the continent to the west much easier.

President Jefferson wanted to find that network of rivers, which people back then called the Northwest Passage. Once the Louisiana Purchase was complete, he sent explorers named Meriwether Lewis (1774–1809) and William Clark (1770–1838) on an expedition to find the passage *and* to explore the new lands the United States had just bought from France.

Lewis and Clark, along with a crew of explorers, started their journey at the mouth of the Missouri River (where it flows into the Mississippi) on May 14, 1804. The expedition, called the Corps of Discovery, followed the Missouri River west.

As they traveled, Clark carefully mapped the route while Lewis collected specimens of animals and plants to send back to Washington, DC. It was an extremely difficult trip. The men in Lewis and Clark's team rowed their three boats against the sometimes heavy Missouri River current and often had to get out of the boats to tow them from the riverbanks when the current became too treacherous. Even on a good day, the Corps of Discovery traveled only 13 or 14 miles.

Over the next several months, the party came in contact with several Indian tribes. All of the natives were friendly except the Lakota Sioux, who lived in what is now South Dakota.

In late August and early September, the party reached the Great Plains, a huge expanse of grasslands that covers parts of present-day Colorado,

HISTORIC HAPPENINGS

On March 1, 1803, Ohio became the seventeenth state in the union. After Congress passed the Northwest Ordinance, the first permanent settlement in Ohio was established in 1788, in Marietta, the capital of the Northwest Territory. In the 1790s, the settlers fought many violent battles with the Native Americans living in the area.

Kansas, Wyoming, Nebraska, New Mexico, North Dakota, South Dakota, Texas, and Wyoming. Along the way, they saw amazing numbers of animals, including huge herds of wild buffalo.

In October 1804, Lewis and Clark decided to stop and build a fort—Fort Mandan—so they could spend the winter in what is now North Dakota. The following spring, they ordered a few of their men to head back down the river to take soil samples, minerals, plants, and some live animals (including some birds and a prairie dog) back to President Jefferson. The rest of the expedition continued up the Missouri River in canoes. When they reached what is now the state of Montana, they found the river too difficult to pass in canoes, so they bought some horses from the Shoshones and continued their journey on horseback.

HiSTORY MAKERS

During the winter of 1804, Lewis and Clark hired a French-Canadian explorer and fur trader named Toussaint Charbonneau (1767–1843) and a Shoshone woman named Sacagawea (c. 1788–1812) to join their expedition. Sacagawea became a very important part of the expedition because she served as an interpreter between the party and the natives who lived near the headwaters of the Missouri River.

What Northwest Passage?

As they headed west from Montana, Lewis and Clark soon realized there was no Northwest Passage to discover. The Corps of Discovery carried maps showing the Missouri River and Columbia River systems separated only by a "ridge of hills" that would take a half a day to pass. What they found instead was a range of mountains—the Bitterroot Range, which is part of the Rocky Mountains—that took two weeks to cross.

It was September 1805 when the party reached the Bitterroots, but the mountains were already covered with snow. By the time the party crossed the mountains and reached present-day Weippe, Idaho, Lewis and Clark and their men hadn't eaten in days and were so weak they were barely able to walk. Fortunately, the Nez Percé Indians who lived in the area were very friendly to them. They welcomed them

LEWIS AND CLARK TRAIL

The Gateway Arch in St. Louis was built to honor America's westward expansion.

and fed them, helped them make canoes for the next part of their journey, and agreed to take care of their horses until they returned on their way back east.

The expedition traveled downstream on the Clearwater, Snake, and Columbia Rivers in canoes. On November 15, 1805—a year and a half after they had started the journey—they reached the mouth of the Columbia River, where it flows into the Pacific Ocean. They built a fort on the south side of the river—near present-day Astoria, Oregon—and named it Fort Clatsop, after a nearby Indian tribe. They spent a cold, wet, windy winter in the fort before starting their trip back home.

Though Lewis and Clark didn't find a northwest passage to the Pacific (it simply didn't exist), their expedition wasn't a failure. They found the source of the Missouri River and had gathered a lot of information about the people, plants, animals, and geography of the places they saw. Lewis and Clark's discoveries helped make it possible for the United States of America to expand to the Pacific coast.

The War of 1812

The War of 1812, which lasted from 1812 to 1815, is sometimes called the Revolutionary War, Part II. That's because it was another war between the United States and Great Britain fought on the North American continent and because it ended with a victory for the Americans.

There were several reasons war broke out between the United States and Great Britain in 1812. First of all, the British had imposed a series of restrictions that hindered trade between the United States and France, which was also at war with the English at the time. Second, the English military practiced "impressment," which meant forcing American sailors to serve in the Royal Navy. Third, the British had been helping American Indian tribes that had been violently resisting the Americans' westward expansion.

President Jefferson wanted to keep American trade with overseas countries going, but he also wanted to keep America out of foreign wars. Jefferson tried to reason with the British, but when that didn't work, he and Congress passed the Embargo Act of 1807, which kept American ships from sailing not just to British and French ports, but to all foreign ports.

Jefferson hoped the Embargo Act would hurt the British and French worse than it hurt the United States and that England would release its trade restrictions on France. But the Embargo Act wound up hurting American traders, whose goods sat in American ports. France and Britain, on the other hand, got along fine without receiving American goods.

In 1808 James Madison was elected as the fifth president of the United States. Before Thomas Jefferson left office, he signed a bill to repeal the Embargo Act. Meanwhile, the American public grew angrier and angrier because the British kept boarding American ships and forcing American sailors to serve in the British Royal Navy.

HISTORIC HAPPENINGS

On June 22, 1807, the crew of the British warship HMS *Leopard* attacked and boarded an American warship, the *Chesapeake*. The attack killed three aboard the *Chesapeake* and injured 18, including the ship's captain, James Barron. Even though this incident, the *Chesapeake-Leopard* Affair, didn't lead the United States directly into war with the British, many historians believe it was a factor in starting the War of 1812. That's because the American public was outraged by the incident and wanted something done about it.

This Means War!

The people who wanted war with Great Britain at that time were called war hawks. Two of the most influential war hawks were Henry Clay, who had represented Kentucky in both the Senate and the House of Representatives, and John C. Calhoun, a politician from South Carolina. In 1812 they persuaded President

Madison to ask Congress for a declaration of war against Great Britain. Madison asked for the declaration and Congress gave it to him.

The United States lost the first "battle" of the War of 1812 without a shot being fired. Soldiers under the command of General William Hull crossed the border from Fort Detroit into Canada. At first, Hull knew he had the Canadian troops, who were serving under British commander Isaac Brock, badly outnumbered. But instead of attacking, Hull waited. After a while, he became convinced *he* was outnumbered and retreated to Fort Detroit then surrendered.

Despite the defeat at Fort Detroit, and despite the fact the British burned the White House, the Capitol, and other buildings in Washington, DC, in the Battle of Washington, the Americans defeated the British in the War of 1812. From September 12–15, 1814, the two sides met in the last official battle of the war, the Battle of Baltimore. Once that battle was finished, the British realized they didn't have enough soldiers left to keep fighting the Americans and the French at the same time. On December 24, 1814, representatives from both sides met in Ghent (modern-day Belgium) and signed the Treaty of Ghent, which officially ended the War of 1812.

Unfortunately, the fighting didn't stop, even after the Treaty of Ghent was signed. In those days, communications traveled slowly and word of the treaty wouldn't reach the United States for weeks. On January 8, 1815, American troops fighting under General Andrew Jackson defeated the British at the Battle of New Orleans. That day, about 2,000 British troops died in a war that was already over.

The Indian Wars

Americans moving west faced all kinds of obstacles as they made their homes in new and unknown places. They had to navigate through sometimes rough terrain and bad weather to do it.

One of the biggest difficulties these pioneers faced was hostility from the people who already lived in the lands they wanted to settle—the American Indians, or Native Americans. Fighting between American settlers and Native American tribes began as far back as the colonial days and lasted through the end of the 1800s. These battles have come to be known as the Indian Wars.

The natives who lived in North America before Europeans settled here lived in groups called tribes. There were many Indian tribes throughout North America, and each had its own culture, beliefs, and lifestyles. Throughout US history, starting in the colonial period, many Indian tribes fought with European settlers and with their descendants. Between the settlement of Jamestown in the early seventeenth century (the 1600s) and the end of the nineteenth century (the 1800s), there were literally dozens of Indian Wars.

From the early 1800s on, as Americans moved west in larger numbers, they encountered hostile natives who wanted to defend the lands they lived and hunted on. When Indian tribes came into contact with the American pioneers or with the US military, it often resulted in one of many Indian Wars fought during the nineteenth century. Here is a list of some of those wars and battles:

1832—The Black Hawk War in northern Illinois and southwestern Wisconsin

1849–1863—The Navajo conflicts in Arizona and New Mexico

1854–1890—The Sioux Wars in Wyoming, Minnesota, and South Dakota

1855–1856—The Rogue River War in southwestern Oregon

1861–1900—The Apache attacks in New Mexico, Arizona, Texas, and Mexico

1865–1868 and **1879**—The Ute Wars in Utah

1872–1873—The Modoc War in northern California and southern Oregon

1874–1875—The Red River War in northwestern Texas

1876—Battle of Rosebud in Rosebud Creek in southern Montana

1876—Battle of the Little Bighorn in southern Montana

1877—The Nez Percé War in Oregon, Idaho, and Montana

1890—The Massacre at Wounded Knee in South Dakota

HISTORY MAKERS

Tashunka Witko (1842–1877), better known as Crazy Horse, was a Lakota Sioux chief remembered as a fierce warrior who earned the respect and fear of the United States Army during the Sioux Wars. Crazy Horse led a war party at the Battle of the Little Bighorn in June 1876. After Crazy Horse surrendered to US troops in 1877, he was fatally wounded by a military guard.

The longest and bloodiest of the Indian Wars was actually a series of wars between the Sioux Indians and the US military called the Sioux Wars. The Sioux lived on the Great Plains in the middle part of the United States, and they depended on buffalo for their food.

When large waves of settlers and prospectors crossed the Mississippi River and started passing through and settling in the plains, many started killing the huge herds of buffalo living there. Sioux warriors, including chiefs such as Sitting Bull and Crazy Horse, tried to protect their hunting grounds. That led to the Sioux Wars, which started in 1854 and ended in December 1890 with the Massacre at Wounded Knee.

The Texas Revolution

The story of how Texas became part of the United States starts in the early 1830s, when thousands of Americans began settling in Texas, a huge territory with a lot of farmland and other natural resources. By 1835 about 30,000 Americans and 8,000 Mexicans lived in Texas. The Americans living there wanted Texas to become part of the United States. The problem was that most of Texas at the time was part of Mexico.

The Alamo, San Antonio, Texas

In 1835 several battles broke out between the Texians (*Texian* was a term for American settlers in what was then northern Mexico) and Mexican soldiers. In December of that year, Texas formally declared itself independent from Mexico. The president of this new republic was a man named Sam Houston, and his secretary of state was Stephen F. Austin, one of the leaders of American settlements in the Texas territory.

Mexico's first major action following Texas's declaration of independence began on February 23, 1836, at the Alamo, a Texian-controlled fort near present-day San Antonio. The Texians fought bravely to defend the Alamo, but by the time the siege ended on March 6, 1836, a total of 189 had died—including famous Americans such as Jim Bowie and Davy Crockett. Mexico was victorious and now controlled the fort.

On March 20, 1836, the Mexican army, under the command of General José de Urrea, defeated Republic of Texas forces at the Battle of Coleto Creek. Following that battle, Mexican general Antonio López de Santa Anna

HISTORY MAKERS

David (Davy) Crockett (1786–1836) was a famous nineteenth-century frontiersman, politician, and soldier. Crockett served in the Tennessee state legislature starting in 1821, and in 1826 he was elected to represent Tennessee in the United States House of Representatives. He also served in the Texas Revolution.

ordered the massacre of 342 American prisoners, including their commander, Colonel James Fannin. This terrible event was called the Goliad Massacre.

A lot of Texians and other Americans were outraged at Santa Anna's cruelty in both of these battles, and many joined the Texian army to fight against Santa Anna's forces. On April 21, 1836, several hundred Texians defeated the much larger Mexican army at the Battle of San Jacinto, in present-day Harris County, Texas.

That battle ended the Texas Revolution. The Republic of Texas was now an independent nation, which extended in parts of present-day New Mexico, Oklahoma, Kansas, Colorado, and Wyoming. The Texas Republic remained independent until it joined the United States of America in 1845.

The Mexican-American War

HISTORIC HAPPENINGS

On March 3, 1845, before the outbreak of the Mexican-American War, Florida became the twenty-seventh state in the union. Spanish settlers had colonized Florida early on, but Spain lost control of the territory after the French and Indian War. Spain regained control of Florida after the Revolutionary War, but sold it to the United States in 1819.

Even though tensions between Texas and Mexico continued after the Texas Revolution, the two sides were mostly at peace for the next nine years. That changed in 1845, when the United States annexed Texas and it became the twenty-eighth state in the union.

After Texas became a part of the United States, border disputes with Mexico became a source of conflict. On April 25, 1846, a clash between Mexican and American soldiers became a war between the two countries. Battles in the Mexican-American War were fought in Texas, New Mexico, and California in the north, and in northern, central, and eastern Mexico, and in Mexico City in the south. When the US Army captured the Mexican capital, Mexico City, in September 1847, the war was all but over.

The Mexican-American War officially ended on February 2, 1848, when both sides signed the Treaty of Guadalupe Hidalgo. In the treaty, Mexico agreed to give up more than half of its territory in exchange for $15 million. The land Mexico gave up to the United States was called the Mexican Cession, and it included all of present-day California,

Nevada, and Utah as well as parts of Arizona, Colorado, New Mexico, and Wyoming.

The United States gained nearly 30,000 more square miles of land from Mexico in 1853, when US ambassador to Mexico James Gadsden negotiated the purchase of land in what is now southern Arizona and southwestern New Mexico. This transaction is known as the Gadsden Purchase. Franklin Pierce, the fourteenth president of the United States, wanted the land because he thought it would be a good place to construct a southern transcontinental railway.

Westward Expansion: America's "Obvious Fate"

One of the United States' motivations for westward expansion in the 1830s and 1840s was a belief that came to be known as Manifest Destiny—which means "obvious fate." Many Americans believed that God had chosen the United States to expand "from sea to shining sea," including places such as Texas, California, and Oregon.

The term "manifest destiny" first appeared in an editorial in the July/August 1845 edition of the *United States Magazine and Democratic Review*. The article was published anonymously, but it has been attributed to editor John L. O'Sullivan. O'Sullivan wrote that it was America's "manifest destiny to overspread the continent allotted by Providence for the free development of our multiplying millions." O'Sullivan was referring specifically to the planned annexation of Texas, but he also stated that God had chosen America to become the superpower of that time and that this could be accomplished by expanding westward and establishing civilization in places that were occupied only by American Indian tribes.

Manifest Destiny caught on in America, and many newspapers and other media promoted the idea. It never became an official policy of the US government, but it greatly influenced many American politicians. One of

HISTORY MAKERS

Zachary Taylor (1784–1850) was the twelfth president of the United States (1849–1850) and an American military general who led American soldiers to victories over Mexican troops in the Battle of Palo Alto and the Battle of Monterrey in the Mexican-American War. Taylor, who had a 40-year military career, was known as Old Rough and Ready. On July 9, 1850, President Taylor died in office under mysterious circumstances.

HISTORIC HAPPENINGS

Between the beginning of the Texas Revolution and the end of the Mexican-American War, five more states were admitted to the union, bringing the total to 29. Arkansas became a state on June 15, 1836, followed by Michigan (January 26, 1837), Florida (March 3, 1845), Texas (December 29, 1845), and Iowa (December 28, 1846). Wisconsin became a state on May 29, 1848, bringing the total to 30.

the results was the Homestead Act of 1862, which encouraged Americans to move west and establish homes and colonies.

Another Spiritual Awakening

As Americans moved west, a second big spiritual revival began to take place. In Chapter 2, you read about the First Great Awakening, which took place during colonial times. The movement known as the Second Great Awakening began early in the 1800s and lasted until the 1840s—though most of it took place during the 1820s and 1830s.

Where the preaching during the First Great Awakening focused mostly on people who were already in church, the work of many preachers and other spiritual leaders during the Second Great Awakening focused on people who didn't go to church. Preachers and teachers such as Charles G. Finney, Lyman Beecher, and Barton Stone spoke to large crowds at "revival meetings."

Even though some Christian leaders opposed what happened during the Second Great Awakening, it led to many thousands of conversions to Christianity and also to the growth of denominations such as the Methodists and Baptists.

As a result of the Second Great Awakening, many American Christians began to work to change their society. They became more aware of things that were wrong in America—such as slavery, the abuse of alcohol, and denying equal rights to women—and they believed it was their duty as Christians to fix as many of those wrongs as they could.

HISTORY MAKERS

Harriet Beecher Stowe (1811–1896) was an important American author and abolitionist and the daughter of antislavery preacher Lyman Beecher. In 1852, she wrote her best-known novel, *Uncle Tom's Cabin*, which described life for African Americans living under slavery. Millions of Americans read the novel or saw the play, and it motivated the antislavery movement in the North and angered proslavery people in the South. Stowe wrote more than 20 books, but *Uncle Tom's Cabin* is by far the best known and most influential.

One of the wrongs many Christians, especially those living in the northeast states, wanted to fix was slavery. Many Christians already believed that slavery was wrong, but after the Second Great Awakening, more and more Christians began to see that owning other human beings against their will and forcing them to work for no pay was a terrible sin against God and against the enslaved people.

Not only did these Christians see that it was a sin to own slaves, they also believed that even *tolerating* slavery in their nation was a sin. That led to a growing "abolitionist movement," which called for the immediate elimination of slavery in the United States.

Hundreds of antislavery groups were formed during this time in American history. While the men in these groups gave speeches and wrote antislavery literature, the women worked to raise money and collect signatures to petition Congress to abolish slavery in the United States immediately. Many of the antislavery groups worked together, hoping to achieve their goal of abolishing slavery in every state of the union, not just in the North.

Compromises—Over Slavery

It might be hard to believe that there was a time when a lot of people in America actually *owned* slaves—when they bought and sold other human beings and forced them to work without pay on farms and in households—under sometimes terrible conditions.

Sadly, though, it's true. Slavery was a common practice in North America starting in the early colonial period. In fact, even some of the Founding Fathers owned slaves. But as time went on, people began to realize it was wrong for one human being to "own" another.

In 1780, just four years after the colonies declared their independence from Great Britain and formed the United States of America, Pennsylvania became the first state to pass laws that would eventually make slavery illegal. By 1850, very few people in the Northern states owned slaves. In the South, however, slavery continued to grow as a source of labor for jobs that required a lot of handwork—such as harvesting cotton and tobacco, two major crops in the South.

The issue of slavery deeply divided the Northern states from those in the South. That division only got worse when Missouri became a state in 1818. The settlers of Missouri wanted slavery to be legal in their state. However, members of Congress from the North didn't want another "slave state" admitted to the union.

This disagreement led to the Missouri Compromise, which Congress passed in 1820. The Missouri Compromise allowed Missouri to be a "slave state" and Maine to join the union as a "free state."

But the issue of slavery in the United States was far from settled. The Missouri Compromise meant that some states would still have legalized slavery while others would not, and that angered many people on both sides of the issue. The compromise also divided the United States with a line that ran across the country from the East Coast to the Pacific Ocean, with slave states to the south and free states to the north.

The deep division over the issue of slavery eventually led to another compromise.

The Compromise of 1850

Thirty years after the Missouri Compromise, California asked to join the United States. The problem was that the Missouri Compromise would have divided California in half, with slavery legal in the south and illegal in the north. Making the problem even more complicated was that part of the territory held by Texas (a slave state) at the time was north of the line that separated slave states from free states.

These issues together created such division in the United States that many people feared a civil war would soon break out. But on January 29, 1850, a senator from Kentucky named Henry Clay offered a solution. Clay made these suggestions:

That Texas give up the land north of the line separating free states from slave states in exchange for $10 million, which it could use to pay off the remaining debt it owed Mexico following the Mexican-American War.

That California be admitted as a "free state."

That the territories of New Mexico (which included present-day Arizona at the time) and Utah be organized without mentioning slavery, meaning the people who lived there would decide the issue of slavery for themselves.

Adoption of the Fugitive Slave Act, which required all US citizens—North and South—to help in the return of runaway slaves.

The slave trade—but not slavery itself—would be made illegal in the District of Columbia, meaning slave owners there could keep their slaves.

At first, Clay's bills failed to pass Congress. And even if they had passed, President Zachary Taylor likely would have vetoed them. But in the fall of 1850, after Taylor died suddenly in office, Senator Stephen Douglas of Illinois helped push through the bills, which new president Millard Fillmore signed in September of that year.

Even though the Compromise of 1850 kept the nation from splitting in two, the issue of slavery continued to divide the country. Over the next decade, the division grew even wider. It was only a matter of time before they led to all-out war between the North and the South. ✖

CHAPTER 5

A Divided Nation

The Civil War and Reconstruction

Even though the Missouri Compromise and the Compromise of 1850 kept the nation from a war between the states—at least for a while—no one on either side of the slavery issue was satisfied. Those who favored legalized slavery didn't think it was right for the federal government to keep people from holding slaves, and those who opposed slavery saw the practice as sinful and unjust and wanted it outlawed in every state in the nation.

Looking back, we can see that a compromise on the issue of slavery was never going to work, because both sides were equally certain they were right. We can also see that it was only a matter of time before war broke out over the issue.

Finally, in 1861, the Civil War, or War Between the States, began. During four long years of fighting, more than 600,000 American soldiers died with more than 400,000 wounded. Some people believe that more than a million civilians died during the war. It has also been estimated that one in ten Northern men between the ages of 20 and 45 and three in ten Southern men between the ages of 18 and 40 died in the war.

iNTERESTiNG!

One issue that divided the North and South was taxes. Goods brought into the United States from foreign countries were subject to a tax called a tariff. Many people in the South believed the tariffs weren't fair, since the Southern states imported a lot more goods than the Northern states. Also, the way the Southerners saw it, the federal government was imposing taxes on goods produced in the South—such as cotton, sugar, and rice—but not on goods produced in the North.

Why the Civil War Happened

If you were to ask most Americans why the Civil War happened, they would probably give you a simple answer: *slavery*. The North and the South went to war because the people in the South wanted to continue enslaving people to do their agricultural work, while people in the North believed slavery was wrong and immoral and that it shouldn't be allowed in a civilized country founded on the idea that God created all people equal.

In a sense, the issue of slavery was the "last straw" that led to the Civil War. But differences between the South and the North dated all the way back to the end of the Revolutionary War. Between 1787 and 1861, the North and the South had drifted apart in just about every way. Their politics were different, their economies were different, and their cultures were different.

One of the biggest issues between the North and the South in the years before the Civil War was what is called "states' rights." The South believed that state laws should carry more weight than federal laws, and when there was a disagreement between the two, states' rights should win out.

This issue of states' rights became even more important because, over the years, the populations of Northern and Midwestern states were growing far more rapidly than those in the South. That meant that the South lost a lot of its political power in Washington, DC, because areas with higher populations have more representation in Congress than those with lower populations.

In the years leading up to the Civil War, people started talking about the different "sections" of the United States. This is called *sectionalism*, and it led to a lot of anger and division within the United States. Before anyone knew it, the nation that had united itself to fight the British in the Revolutionary War had become a nation divided by sectional differences.

Why Did the South Still Want Slaves?

By the middle of the nineteenth century, the Northern states had pretty much ended the practice of slavery in their states. In the South, however, slavery had become a normal part of everyday life. But why

did people in the South continue using slaves when people in the North had mostly stopped the practice? There are several reasons.

At first, the economy of the United States was built mostly on agriculture—the growing, harvesting, and buying and selling of goods produced on farms. But during the early 1800s, the North's economy changed and became more based on industry— making and selling things produced in factories—than on agriculture. In the South, however, the economy remained based almost completely on agriculture.

In the 1800s, most people in the South were farmers who made their money growing crops such as cotton, rice, sugarcane, and tobacco on big farms called plantations. To make their plantations more profitable, the owners needed cheap labor to do the work of planting, cultivating, and harvesting their crops.

The plantation owners relied on slaves to provide that labor. Some slaves worked in the fields, and some worked processing the crops for sale. Others did household chores in the plantation owners' homes.

Arguments over Slavery

Many Northerners didn't like the fact that slavery was growing and expanding in the South. They saw the practice as uncivilized and immoral. Some wanted slavery limited, while many others wanted to see it outlawed completely.

People in the Southern states argued that slavery had been a part of their way of life for more than two centuries and that it was protected by state and federal laws. They also argued that the US Constitution guaranteed their right to own property and be protected from the illegal seizure of that property. Since slaves were considered property in the South at that time, the Southerners argued that the federal government had no business telling them they couldn't practice slavery.

For decades, the South's distrust of the Northern states had been growing and getting worse. Southerners believed that no one in Congress

HISTORY MAKERS

John Brown (1800–1859) was an American abolitionist whose radical (harsh and extreme) approach toward making slavery illegal led to his execution. While most abolitionists used peaceful tactics to help outlaw slavery, Brown believed in and practiced violence to get his antislavery views across. In 1856 he led the Pottawatomie Massacre, which resulted in the deaths of five men in Kansas. He also attempted an unsuccessful raid on a Virginia military armory in 1859. As a result, Brown was convicted of murder and treason against the state of Virginia and executed for his crimes.

would listen to their concerns. Leaders in some Southern states talked openly of separating from the United States and forming their own government.

The Election of Abraham Lincoln

In 1860 Abraham Lincoln's election as the sixteenth president of the United States only made the division between North and South worse. Southerners already believed that the federal government was interfering too much in their affairs, and they didn't think Lincoln would treat them fairly. That's because Lincoln was a member of the Republican Party, which many saw as friendly to abolitionists and Northern businessmen. Lincoln had also promised to keep the country united and to keep the new Western territories free of slavery.

For some of the Southern states, it was a simple choice: they would secede (break away) from the United States and form their own government. Lincoln thought their threats were a bluff and that the Southerners would never seriously consider leaving the union. But not long after Lincoln's election, Southern political leaders began calling for statewide votes to consider secession.

In December 1860, after Lincoln's election but before he took office, South Carolina became the first Southern state to secede from the United States. On February 4, 1861, Georgia, Florida, Alabama, Mississippi, and Louisiana joined South Carolina in a new nation called the Confederate States of America (the Confederacy for short), and Texas joined a month later. After the start of the Civil War, Virginia, Arkansas, North Carolina, and Tennessee also joined the Confederacy.

At the initial Confederate States Convention, Jefferson Davis, a Democratic senator from Mississippi and a champion of states' rights, was appointed as temporary president of the Confederacy. On November 6, 1861, Davis was formally elected after running unopposed.

> **iNTERESTiNG!**
>
> Even though the state of Virginia broke away from the United States and joined the Confederacy in 1861, people living in the western counties of Virginia didn't want to secede with the rest of the state. On June 20, 1863, this part of Virginia became a state of its own, called West Virginia.

Heading Toward a Civil War

President Lincoln had declared that he was willing to do whatever it took to keep the Southern states as part of the United States. Even after South Carolina led a parade of Southern states in seceding, there were Union forts in Confederate territory. The Confederates wanted the Union soldiers to leave the forts, and when

Lincoln's predecessor, President James Buchanan, refused to surrender the forts, troops from the Southern states began taking them by force.

The Confederates warned Union soldiers to leave Fort Sumter, which sits at the entrance to the Charleston Harbor in South Carolina. When the Union troops refused to leave, on April 12, 1861, the Confederate States of America fired cannons at the fort. The attack lasted several hours. No one was killed or injured, but the fort was badly damaged. Rather than fight a battle he knew he couldn't win, Union Major Robert Anderson surrendered and allowed Confederate commanders to take control of the fort and its weapons.

Up to this point, the war between the South and North was mostly a war of words. But with the attack on Fort Sumter, the Civil War had begun.

President Lincoln, who had done everything he could to avoid a war, responded to the attack on Fort Sumter by calling for volunteers from states still loyal to the union to help deal with this treasonous act on the part of the Confederacy. This led to the secession of the final four states to join the Confederacy: Virginia, Arkansas, North Carolina, and Tennessee.

> ### INTERESTING!
> Even though Delaware, Kentucky, Maryland, and Missouri were "slave states"—meaning states where slavery was still legal—they did not join the Confederacy. They were persuaded to stay in the union through a combination of political strategy and Union military pressure.

This Shouldn't Take Too Long!

At the start of the Civil War, most people didn't believe it would last very long. Some even believed the war would last only a few months and that before long, Union soldiers would be welcomed home as conquering heroes.

The North had several advantages over the South at the beginning of the Civil War. They were far better off financially, producing about 75 percent of the nation's wealth, and they had a bigger army with much better weapons and supplies.

But the South had some advantages of its own, starting with the fact that most of the war would be fought on Southern territory. That meant the Confederate soldiers were defending their own land.

Both sides asked their states to raise companies of volunteer soldiers to fight. Tens of thousands of young men in both the North and the South enlisted. The men in the South wanted to protect their homes and their way of life, and the men in the North wanted to defeat the Southern states, bring the nation back together, and teach the rebellious South a lesson it wouldn't forget. Some of the Northern volunteer soldiers wanted to fight to abolish slavery.

Lincoln's New Goal

WORTH REPEATING

"There is no reason in the world why the negro is not entitled to all the natural rights enumerated in the Declaration of Independence, the right to life, liberty, and the pursuit of happiness. I hold that he is as much entitled to these as the white man."
—Abraham Lincoln, 1858

HISTORIC HAPPENINGS

Even though President Lincoln's Emancipation Proclamation freed most slaves living in the United States, the final abolition of slavery did not happen until 1865, when Congress passed the Thirteenth Amendment to the United States Constitution, which read, "Neither slavery nor involuntary servitude, except as a punishment for crime whereof the party shall have been duly convicted, shall exist within the United States, or any place subject to their jurisdiction." This amendment was ratified by the states on December 6, 1865.

At the beginning of the Civil War, President Lincoln declared that the North was fighting the war to save the union, not to end slavery. But about a year after the war began, he changed his position. It was then that he wrote a document called the Emancipation Proclamation, which freed slaves in all the states that had left the union and joined the Confederacy.

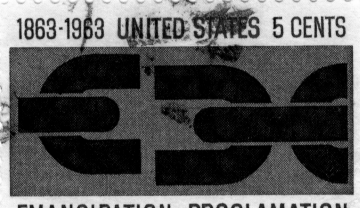

On September 22, 1862, Lincoln issued a formal declaration of emancipation (which means freedom) of all slaves in the Confederate states that refused to return to the union by January 1, 1863. When none of the states returned, Lincoln formally issued the Emancipation Proclamation.

The Emancipation Proclamation had several effects. First, it granted freedom to all slaves in the Confederate states. Second, it made the abolition of slavery one of the main goals of the war. Third, it made it possible for African American soldiers to serve in the Union Army and Navy. Finally, it made it impossible for England and France, European countries that were opposed to slavery, to help the Confederacy in its war effort.

How the Union Won the Civil War

The Union Army quickly took control of the border states—Delaware, Kentucky, Maryland, and Missouri—which were slave states that had not seceded from the Union before April 1861. The Union Navy also placed a naval blockade on coastal Confederate states. This kept them from exporting cotton, which they depended on for their wealth and for money to fight the war.

In 1861 and 1862, neither side gained much ground from the other. The Confederacy stopped the Union from capturing its capital city of Richmond, Virginia. On June 13, 1863, Confederate General Robert E. Lee defeated Union forces in a battle at Winchester, Virginia, and then decided it was time to lead his men north into Pennsylvania.

After the victory at Winchester, the Confederates were confident they could defeat the Union Army by invading the North. Lee marched his men to Gettysburg, Pennsylvania, where they fought against the Union soldiers in a three-day battle called the Battle of Gettysburg.

WORTH REPEATING

"I tremble for my country when I hear of confidence expressed in me. I know too well my weakness, that our only hope is in God."
—Robert E. Lee, Confederate general

HISTORIC HAPPENINGS

On November 19, 1863, President Lincoln gave one of the best—and most important—speeches in US history. He delivered the speech at Gettysburg, Pennsylvania, the place where the Battle of Gettysburg took place. Maybe you've heard the first line of Lincoln's famous speech: "Four score and seven years ago our fathers brought forth on this continent, a new nation, conceived in liberty, and dedicated to the proposition that all men are created equal." You can read President Lincoln's whole speech in Appendix C (page 153).

THE GETTYSBURG ADDRESS

DELIVERED BY ABRAHAM LINCOLN NOV. 19 1863 — AT THE DEDICATION SERVICES ON THE BATTLE FIELD

Fourscore and seven years ago our fathers brought forth on this continent a new nation, conceived in liberty, and dedicated to the proposition that all men are created equal. ★ ★ ★ Now we are engaged in a great civil war, testing whether that nation, or any nation so conceived and so dedicated, can long endure. ★ ★ We are met on a great battle-field of that war. ★ We have come to dedicate a portion of that field as a final resting place for those who here gave their lives that that nation might live. ★ ★ It is altogether fitting and proper that we should do this. ★ ★ But in a larger sense we cannot dedicate, we cannot consecrate, we cannot hallow this ground. ★ The brave men, living and dead, who struggled here, have consecrated it far above our poor power to add or detract. The world will little note, nor long remember, what we say here, but it can never forget what they did here. ★ ★ It is for us, the living, rather to be dedicated here to the unfinished work which they who fought here have thus far so nobly advanced It is rather for us to be here dedicated to the great task remaining before us, that from these honored dead we take increased devotion to that cause for which they gave the last full measure of devotion; ★ that we here highly resolve that these dead shall not have died in vain: that this nation, under God, shall have a new birth of freedom, and that the government of the people, by the people, and for the people, shall not perish from the earth

PUBLISHED AND COPYRIGHT 1905 BY M.T. SHEAHAN, BOSTON, MASS.

The Battle of Gettysburg, which was fought between July 1 and July 3, 1863, was one of the most important battles in the Civil War. It was also the bloodiest, with close to 51,000 casualties, including nearly 8,000 deaths.

On the first day of the battle, Lee's men outnumbered the Union soldiers, and the Union was forced to retreat from battle to the south side of the town of Gettysburg. General Lee wanted to finish the battle then and there, but his men delayed their attack, giving the Union time to set up its defenses and prepare to fight again the next day.

On the second day of fighting, both armies were at full strength. Lee attacked the Union Army, but they held their position. On the third day, Lee sent General George Pickett and 12,500 men to launch what he hoped would be the deciding attack in the battle—and in the war itself. In what has since been called Pickett's Charge, the general led his men on a direct attack against the Union Army. But more than half of Pickett's men were either killed or injured in the charge, forcing General Lee and the Confederate Army to retreat.

The Union Army, led by General George Meade, might have ended the war that day if he had pursued the retreating Confederate soldiers. But his men were exhausted by the fighting and did not pursue General Lee's troops. General Meade was later criticized, but he deserves credit for helping to save the Union.

The Battle of Gettysburg turned out to be a major turning point in the war for the Union. General Lee would never again attempt such a large offensive campaign against the Union. Even though the war continued for two more years, the Confederacy never recovered from its decisive defeat at Gettysburg.

The Beginning of the End for the Confederacy

On the morning of April 9, 1865, General Lee's Army of Northern Virginia met with General Ulysses S. Grant's Union Army for the final time in the war, in the Battle of Appomattox Court House. It was also one of the last battles of the Civil War.

Lee soon realized that his forces were outnumbered and that he had no choice but to surrender. That afternoon, he met with Grant at a house owned by Wilmer McLean, a grocer and former officer in the Virginia militia, to sign formal documents of surrender.

As Lee left McLean's house, mounted his horse, and rode away, Grant's men cheered in celebration. Grant, however, ordered them to stop their cheering. "The Confederates were now our countrymen," he later said, "and we did not want to exult over their downfall."

On April 12, the Army of Northern Virginia was disbanded and its officers and soldiers were given amnesty and allowed to return to their homes.

While some people celebrated the end of the war, General Grant knew there were still about 175,000 Confederate soldiers in the field. But as news of Lee's surrender spread, most of them laid down their weapons and stopped fighting. By the end of June, the last major Confederate armies had surrendered, ending the war.

The Civil War ended with the Union victorious, the country came back together (after a time, that is), and slavery ended in the United States. But the cost to both sides was staggering. In addition to the horrible loss of life, the South—where most of the war was fought—was devastated in nearly every way.

Now it was time to do the work of rebuilding the South, and of healing and reuniting a nation that had been at war with itself for four years.

Reconstructing the South

A terrible chapter in American history ended when the Union defeated the Confederacy in the Civil War. But that meant a new chapter was just beginning: bringing the nation back together as the United States of America. This part of American history is called the Reconstruction, and it started soon after the Civil War ended and lasted for 12 years, until 1877.

HISTORY MAKERS

Ulysses S. Grant (1822–1885) was the eighteenth president of the United States and a war hero who led the Union Army to victory over the Confederate States of America, which ended the Civil War and the Confederacy. Grant fought in the Mexican-American War, where he served under General Zachary Taylor. After the Civil War broke out, he joined the Union Army, and in 1864 he became the commanding general.

INTERESTING!

During the Civil War, Union and Confederate forces engaged in more than 50 major battles and more than 5,000 minor battles. Civil War battles took place in 23 states (Alabama, Arkansas, Florida, Georgia, Indiana, Kansas, Kentucky, Louisiana, Maine, Maryland, Minnesota, Mississippi, Missouri, New York, North Carolina, Ohio, Pennsylvania, South Carolina, Tennessee, Texas, Vermont, Virginia, and West Virginia) and in the District of Columbia, as well as in the Arizona Territory, the Colorado Territory, the Dakota Territory, the Indian Territory, the New Mexico Territory, and the Washington Territory.

Well before the Civil War ended, the members of Congress argued about the requirements for bringing the Southern states back into the union. Some favored a gentler approach to Reconstruction. They believed that the Union should not punish the South for seceding, but should instead take the steps necessary to heal and unite the nation as a whole. They also believed the federal government should play a limited role in changing the politics and social customs of the South.

Other members of Congress believed the US government should follow a course called Radical Reconstruction, which meant *punishing* the South for seceding and having the federal government more directly involved in the affairs of the Southern states. That included forcing political and social changes on the South that would make it more like the North. It also meant immediately granting the newly freed slaves (also called "freedmen") the same rights and liberties given to Southern white people. These members of Congress believed that if they didn't take that approach, the South would soon go right back to doing what it had done before.

Reconstruction...Lincoln Style

On December 8, 1863, about 16 months before the South surrendered to the North to end the Civil War, President Lincoln presented his vision for Reconstruction. Lincoln knew the Civil War would leave the nation, especially the South, devastated. He wanted to do everything he could to quickly heal the wounds the war had caused and put an end to the divisions between the North and the South.

Lincoln's plan, called the Proclamation of Amnesty and Reconstruction, called for the federal government to appoint governors for the states that had seceded from the union and for pardons for all Southerners who took an oath of support to the US Constitution and the United States of America. This general pardon did not apply to high-ranking Confederate officials, who could only be pardoned by a special order from President Lincoln. A Confederate state could rejoin the union only after 10 percent of its qualified voters took the oath of allegiance.

Lincoln's proclamation didn't help the situation. Some members of Congress believed he was being too soft on the South and that his plan would make it easier for the South to go back to the way it was before the Civil War.

In 1864 Congress passed the Wade-Davis Bill, which said that before a state could rejoin the union, more than half of the state's male voters must take an "ironclad" oath saying they had never voluntarily supported the Confederacy. The Wade-Davis bill also prohibited former Confederate officials from voting or holding office. Lincoln refused to sign the Wade-Davis Bill, meaning it did not become law. Instead, he put his own plan for Reconstruction into effect.

Lincoln's Assassination

On April 14, 1865, five days after Confederate General Robert E. Lee surrendered to Union General Ulysses S. Grant to end the Civil War, a well-known actor named John Wilkes Booth shot President Lincoln as the president watched the play *Our American Cousin* at Ford's Theatre in Washington, DC. Lincoln died the next morning.

Lincoln's assassination was part of a bigger plot by Booth and two other men to kill the president, Vice President Andrew Johnson, and Secretary of State William H. Seward. Booth and his fellow plotters believed that if they killed all three men (who were the top three leaders in the US government), they would rally the Confederate troops to keep fighting and would also throw the

The restored Ford's Theater today.

Union government into chaos. But the plot was only partly successful. Seward was wounded but survived, and the attack on Johnson never happened.

On the day Abraham Lincoln died, he and Congress were nowhere near an agreement over Reconstruction. And for many years after that, the nation remained in turmoil over how to reunify the states.

When Lincoln died, Andrew Johnson became president during the difficult time when the nation wrestled with how to bring all the states back together.

A New National Leader, the Same National Problem

On April 15, 1865, Andrew Johnson became the seventeenth president of the United States. Many people expected him to impose harsher policies toward the former Confederate states than Lincoln would have. But

Johnson agreed with Lincoln that the government should not seek to punish the Southern states, but instead treat them with leniency and forgiveness, so he decided to follow Lincoln's plan for Reconstruction.

On May 29, 1865, President Johnson issued a proclamation forgiving all Southerners (with the exception of a few key Confederate leaders) who took an oath of allegiance to the US Constitution and government. He also appointed temporary governors for the Southern states that were rejoining the union. In time, he pardoned all but a few high-ranking, wealthy Confederates and allowed the state governors he had appointed to appoint former Confederates to office.

Like Lincoln, Johnson didn't believe it was up to the federal government to force states to give the freedmen equal rights, so he left that issue up to the individual state governments. One of Johnson's conditions for a state to rejoin the union was that the state must ratify the Thirteenth Amendment, which abolished (put an end to) slavery. But he refused to use the power of the federal government to enforce the rights of the freedmen.

By the end of 1865, every Southern state but Texas had ratified the Thirteenth Amendment, organized a government, and elected members to Congress. Great strides had been made, and President Johnson declared that the Reconstruction was finished.

But it wasn't.

Back to Radical Reconstruction

Many members of Congress thought Johnson's Reconstruction policies didn't go nearly far enough. They believed that his policies, even though they called for states to ratify the Thirteenth Amendment, led to laws that treated former slaves unequally and also to the election of former Confederates to public office—including to Congress.

Members of Congress who favored Radical Reconstruction wanted to see more social and political change in the South, and they believed the only way for that to happen was for the federal government to command it. Instead of trying to make changes to Johnson's Reconstruction plans, the Congress enacted its own plan.

INTERESTING!

President Andrew Johnson's refusal to use federal power to guarantee equal rights for freed slaves meant that African Americans living in the South would not be treated as equal to their white neighbors. In fact, many Southern states established laws called "black codes," which limited the rights of the freedmen.

HISTORY MAKERS

During the time of Reconstruction, many in the United States Congress objected to the elections of former high-ranking officers of the Confederacy to the House of Representatives or Senate. One of those officers was a man named Alexander Stephens (1812–1883), who had been awaiting trial for treason when Georgia elected him to a seat in the US Senate. Congress barred Stephens (and others with backgrounds like his) from taking his seat, citing a clause in the US Constitution that states, "Each house [the House of Representatives and the Senate] shall be the judge of the qualifications of its own members."

In early April 1866, Congress passed the Civil Rights Act of 1866, which protected freedmen from laws being passed in many Southern states to keep them from enjoying the same rights as white people. This act declared that every person born in the United States "of every race and color" was now a citizen with the same rights as everyone else.

President Johnson vetoed the Civil Rights Act of 1866 because he thought it gave the federal government too much power. Many people were angry at Johnson for vetoing the bill, and Congress quickly voted to override the veto (Congress can set aside a presidential veto with a two-thirds vote of the membership), making it now the law in the United States. It was the first time in US history that Congress had overridden a presidential veto of a bill.

About two years later, on July 9, 1868, Congress ensured that the civil rights bill was enforced when it approved the Fourteenth Amendment, which guaranteed full citizenship rights to the freedmen. Congress also made ratification of this amendment a condition for rejoining the union.

In June 1868, Tennessee and six other Southern states formally rejoined the union. That same year, Congress prepared the Fifteenth Amendment—which prohibited states from denying any American the right to vote based on "race, color, or previous condition of servitude"—and made it a condition for the remaining states to rejoin the union. The rest of the former Confederate states were admitted by the end of 1870. Georgia was the last to be readmitted.

A Big Change at the Top

In 1869 Civil War hero Ulysses S. Grant was elected as the eighteenth president of the United States. Grant supported Congress' Radical Reconstruction plans. Grant was also reelected in

1873. Unfortunately, his presidency did not bring an end to the nation's turmoil over Reconstruction.

By 1870 the Radical Reconstructionists in Congress accomplished several of their goals. On February 3 enough states had ratified the Fifteenth Amendment for it to become law, which gave black people the right to vote. As a result, two African Americans won election to Congress: Senator Hiram Rhodes Revels (from Mississippi) and Representative Joseph Rainey (from South Carolina). In July Georgia became the last former Confederate state to be readmitted to the Union.

The Reconstruction era ended in 1877, the year after Republican Rutherford B. Hayes won a disputed election over Samuel Tilden to become the nineteenth president of the United States. Tilden won the popular vote (meaning more people cast a ballot for him than for Hayes) but lost in the electoral vote. Southern Democrats agreed to support Hayes's election if he would pull all federal troops out of South Carolina, Florida, and Louisiana, where they had helped keep Republicans in control.

This is called the Compromise of 1877, but it has also been called the Corrupt Bargain. Before Hayes took office, President Grant removed the soldiers from Florida, and Hayes removed them from South Carolina and Louisiana. Once the troops left, the Reconstruction era was officially over.

Sadly, the end of Reconstruction meant that many of the gains made by and for the freedmen since the end of the Civil War were reversed. Slavery remained illegal throughout the United States, including in the South, but in many states, former slaves and their children lost a lot of their rights as citizens.

HISTORY MAKERS

Hiram Rhodes Revels (1827–1901) was an African American minister who became the first black man to serve in the United States Senate and the United States Congress. Revels represented Mississippi in 1870 and 1871, during Reconstruction. Earlier, Revels had served as a minister in the African Methodist Episcopal Church and as a chaplain for the US Army. He also helped organize two black Union regiments during the Civil War and took part in the Battle of Vicksburg in Mississippi.

GRANT

The Fifteenth Amendment may have given African Americans, who were the majority in states like Mississippi, Louisiana, and Alabama, the right to vote; but white supremacist groups engaged in intimidation, violence, and sometimes murder to keep blacks from voting. That led to the election to Congress of Southern Democrats—also called Redeemer Democrats—who had opposed the gains the freedman made over the previous few decades.

Starting in 1876 (and lasting until the 1960s), Southern states began passing laws which led to separate public facilities—schools, transportation, restrooms, even drinking fountains—for whites and blacks. The South became more and more segregated, and anger and conflict between whites and blacks grew as a result.

CHAPTER 6

Immigration, Industry, and a Really Big War

The United States after the Civil War

Once the Civil War was over, the United States was again ready to begin growing as a global economic power. And grow it did! After the Civil War, American business and industry grew and expanded so fast that by the end of the nineteenth century, the United States' economy had replaced Great Britain's as the world's largest.

A lot of factors helped make possible America's rapid rise to the top. Those factors included a big increase in the number of people living in the United States, better transportation, and a lot of really cool inventions. (Okay, maybe some of them won't seem so cool to you now, but back then they were a really big deal.)

In this chapter, you'll read about how the United States of America had its own "population explosion" following the Civil War, and how all those new people helped American industry grow throughout the second half of the nineteenth century and the early part of the twentieth century.

You'll also read about how the United States became involved in the first global war in world history: World War I.

Immigration Heats Up in the United States

INTERESTING!

In Ireland a disease that killed potato crops led to a terrible time now called the Great Famine or the Irish Potato Famine. Between 1845 and 1852, the population of Ireland dropped by 2 million people. About half died from starvation and other disease, while the other half left the country to find a better life. Many of those people emigrated to the United States.

The United States of America has often been called a nation of immigrants, and history shows that is true. By the 1820s, every American who wasn't from one of the many Indian tribes throughout the land was either an immigrant or a descendant of immigrants.

Historians estimate that fewer than a million Europeans emigrated to North America during the seventeenth and eighteenth centuries. Immigration to the United States was slow after the Revolutionary War, but the number of people moving to America from other countries gradually increased around the 1820s. Starting in the 1840s, a huge wave of immigrants from Ireland and Germany began arriving on the shores of the United States.

These new immigrants were fleeing their homelands in Europe due to crop failures that led to famines and due to unrest in their native countries. Some historians estimate that between 1847 and 1854, an average of 335,000 people—almost half of them from Ireland—moved to the United States each year.

During the Civil War, immigration from Europe slowed down (after all, who wanted to move to a country being torn apart by war?). But once the Civil War ended, the number of people moving to the United States increased again. Between 1865 and 1873, more than 325,000 Europeans—from Great Britain, Germany, Ireland, and other countries—came to the United States every year.

For the most part, immigration to the United States increased every year after the Civil War. Before the Civil War, immigrants had to travel over the Atlantic Ocean on sailing ships. Many people died during the voyages. But after the war, the introduction of steamships—which were much faster than sailing ships—helped reduce the number of deaths. It also lowered the cost of migrating to North America.

Between 1836 and 1914, more than 30 million Europeans crossed the Atlantic Ocean to come to the United States. In 1907 alone, almost 1.3 million Europeans entered the country. By 1910, 13.5 million out of the 92.4 million people living in the United States were immigrants.

Some of the immigrants came to the United States only to work and make money before they returned home, but many others came to establish new homes in a place where they could make a better life for themselves and their families. While these new immigrants weren't always welcomed with open arms, they helped establish growing industries in the United States such as steel, coal, textiles, garment production, and automobiles. These new workers helped make the United States one of the world's most important countries economically.

INTERESTING!

The construction of the Transcontinental Railroad came after many years of politicking. In 1845 an American businessman named Asa Whitney (1797–1872) approached the US Congress with a plan calling for the federal government to help pay for the construction of a railroad from the Mississippi River to the Pacific coast. In 1853 Congress funded the surveying of potential routes for a railroad to the West Coast. On July 1, 1862—during the Civil War—Congress passed laws providing funds for a transcontinental line. This legislation called for two companies to build the railroad, with each receiving federal land grants and government loans for each mile of track built.

Chinese Immigrants' Big Contribution

In the 1850s, many young men from China left their homeland and migrated to North America to find work. These immigrants were fleeing a country where they couldn't find work and where the government was very unstable. Many ended up in Northern California, which was being settled at that time by people coming west for the gold rush. Most of these Chinese immigrants landed in the port city of San Francisco and then moved to the gold fields in the foothills of the Sierra Nevada mountains. Historians estimate that by the late 1850s, around 15,000 Chinese immigrants worked in California gold mines.

HISTORY MAKERS

Charles Crocker (1822–1888) was a founder of the Central Pacific Railroad and the man most responsible for recruiting immigrants from China to construct a large part of the first Transcontinental Railroad. Many of Crocker's business partners didn't think Chinese workers were big enough or strong enough for the backbreaking work, but Crocker hired them anyway, and they became known as Crocker's Pets. Unfortunately, Crocker treated the Chinese laborers terribly. He worked them to the point of exhaustion and paid them a lot less than his other workers. He also didn't pay for their food or housing.

When the California Gold Rush began to wind down, many of the Chinese immigrants who had worked in the mines started working on one of the most important (maybe *the* most important) construction projects of the 1800s: the first transcontinental railroad, which would provide a railway link between the East Coast and the Pacific.

Two railroad companies, the Union Pacific Railroad and the Central Pacific Railroad, began construction on the Transcontinental Railroad in 1863. The Union Pacific Railroad started in Omaha, Nebraska, and the Central Pacific Railroad started in Sacramento, California. On May 10, 1869, the two sections of railroad finally met at Promontory Summit, Utah. To celebrate the completion of the railroad, a ceremonial golden spike was driven into the final wooden tie by Leland Stanford, president of the Central Pacific Railroad.

Chinese immigrants did most of the work building the Central Pacific part of the first Transcontinental Railroad. These men worked in sometimes terrible conditions and for lower pay than other workers. They worked in the heat of the summer and in the

extreme cold of the winter, and many of them died. They had to lay track on flat land, but they also had to build bridges over canyons and rivers and construct tunnels through the Sierra Nevada and Rocky Mountains. They used dynamite to bore the tunnels, and many workers were killed in the explosions.

Over the next few decades, more railroad lines were built. Three were completed in 1883: The Northern Pacific Railroad, which stretched from Lake Superior to Portland, Oregon; the Santa Fe Railroad, which traveled between Atchison, Kansas, and Los Angeles, California; and the Southern Pacific Railroad, which connected Los Angeles with New Orleans, Louisiana. In 1893 the Great Northern Railway was completed.

How important were these new railroads? Well, before they were completed, people had to travel west in wagon trains, on horseback, or on foot. Americans were traveling west and settling there, but the new railroads made it possible for people to travel west faster and more safely. A trip that once took months and was filled with all sorts of dangers now could be completed safely in a week or less.

Not only that, but people could now transport goods by train, which helped speed up economic expansion in the west and in the east. Before the railroad, trade between the eastern half of the United States and the western half was extremely difficult, if not impossible. But within ten years of the completion of the first Transcontinental Railroad, more than $50 million worth of goods were being shipped from one side of the continent to the other every year.

HISTORY MAKERS

John Pierpont (J. P.) Morgan (1837–1913) was the most important US banker during the rise of American industry in the late 1800s and early 1900s. Morgan supplied huge amounts of money that American businesses needed for expansion. By the early 1900s, he and his business partners had invested in many large corporations in the United States. In 1892 Morgan formed General Electric when he arranged the merger of Edison General Electric and Thomson-Houston Electric Company. He also formed the United States Steel Corporation in 1901.

The Rise of American Industry

In Europe and North America during the 1700s and 1800s, big changes took place in farming, manufacturing, mining, technology, and transportation. These changes were part of what is often called the Industrial Revolution, which transformed the way people produced goods and the way they were sold.

During colonial times, the American economy was based mostly on agriculture. But in the early 1800s, industry began to grow in the United States. That growth continued all the way through the Civil War. But manufacturing was far different back then than it is today. Most manufacturing was done in small shops using hand labor. Most of those businesses served small, local markets.

But once the Civil War was over, American industry began to change very quickly. As more Americans moved west of the Appalachians, they settled in places with a wide variety of natural resources, including trees for lumber; important minerals like iron ore and coal, both of which would play a huge role in manufacturing; and valuable minerals such as copper, silver, and gold.

The rise in American industry was also fueled by a huge increase in the number of people living here following the Civil War. As millions of people immigrated to the United States, a lot of babies were born here as well, and the population jumped from about 40 million people living in the United States in 1870 to almost 102 million in 1916. (If you're good at math, you might have already figured out that the US population increased more than 150 percent in less than 50 years!)

Having all those new people in the United States meant there were more people who wanted and needed the goods American businesses produced, and there were a lot more people available to do the work needed to *produce* those goods.

Another important reason for the expansion of American industry during this time was the development of machines that could do work that once had been done by hand. Mechanized production meant that all those new workers could produce goods much faster, allowing American businesses to produce and sell more products at a lower price. Now many more people could afford to buy the products produced by American industry.

Improvements in transportation—especially the growth of railroads—also helped the US economy to grow. In 1850 there were 9,000 miles of railroad lines operating in the United States; by 1900, that number had increased to nearly 200,000 miles of track. This made it possible for companies to ship their finished and unfinished goods *from* anywhere in the nation *to* anywhere in the nation.

As manufacturing grew in the United States, more and more companies needed money—also called *capital*—to expand their businesses. They got it from two sources: investors and banks. People eager to make money from the new manufacturing boom invested in the companies, which gave these businesses the money they needed to expand. Also, new banks opened all over the country, offering growing businesses low-interest loans to help them expand.

A Time of Invention

American inventors had developed newer and better products throughout the country's history. But the late 1860s was a time when inventors from both the United States and Europe developed amazing numbers of products the American people wanted to buy. Here are just a few products introduced between 1867 and 1879.

1867: Christopher Latham Sholes invented the first practical mechanical typewriter. On June 23, 1868, Sholes's invention was granted a patent (meaning that other people were prohibited from copying and selling their own version of Sholes's device, at least for a certain amount of time). Patents are an important way to protect inventors who invest a lot of time and money developing new products.

1874: Joseph F. Glidden improved an older type of fencing and received a patent for barbed wire.

1876: An inventor named Alexander Graham Bell received a patent for the telephone. Another inventor, Elisha Gray, is also credited with inventing the telephone, but Bell now receives credit for the invention because he patented his phone first.

1877: American inventor Thomas Alva Edison completed his first phonograph, a device used to record and play sounds. Edison's invention used paper—and later metal—cylinders for recording. Subsequent phonographs used vinyl discs, which remained popular until they were replaced by compact digital discs (CDs).

1879: Thomas Edison developed an improved electric light bulb. Edison wasn't the first inventor to introduce electric lighting, but his development made it practical and safe to use electric lighting in homes.

HISTORY MAKERS

Brothers Orville (1871–1948) and Wilbur Wright (1867–1912) were two Americans credited with inventing and building the world's first successful airplane. Other people had built "flying machines" before, but the Wrights' aircraft, called the Wright Flyer, was the first with controls that made fixed-wing powered flight possible. On December 17, 1903, the Wrights flew the Wright Flyer four times near Kill Devil Hills, about four miles south of Kitty Hawk, North Carolina.

How Cars Changed American Life and Industry

In 1885 a German inventor named Karl Benz produced the first gasoline-powered automobile. In 1891 an American named John W. Lambert produced the first gasoline-powered car in the United States.

Probably no invention changed the US economy more than the automobile. Before 1900 only the very well-to-do could afford to buy a car. That began to change in 1902, when Ransom Olds, founder of the Olds Motor Vehicle Company in Lansing, Michigan, began using a manufacturing process called assembly-line production at his company. This form of mass production made Olds's Curved Dash Oldsmobile the first low-priced car in American history.

Starting in 1914, Henry Ford, the founder of Ford Motor Company, added improvements to the assembly-line way of making cars. The results changed not only the automobile industry but other manufacturing around the world as well. Ford's cars came off the assembly line at amazing speed, and the number of injuries at his factories dropped compared to other car makers. That's mostly because his workers stayed in one place on the assembly line all day, rather than moving from place to place.

It wasn't long before most major industries in the United States began copying Ford's assembly-line production techniques. That led to higher productivity and lower production costs in American companies—and to lower prices for the people who bought their goods. Many companies that didn't use assembly-line production, including many car companies, went out of business because they couldn't compete. Those that adapted were able to prosper and grow.

The automobile industry, where mass production using assembly manufacturing got its start, expanded as more and more Americans could afford to buy cars. In 1900 Americans owned a total of only 8,000 cars. By 1916 that number had increased to 3.5 million.

How American Industry Changed America

The rapid growth of manufacturing in the United States affected the nation in many important ways. By 1890 America had become the world's leader in industrial production, passing up longtime leader Great Britain. By the turn of the twentieth century, the United States by far led the world in per capita (per person) income.

These changes in the US economy also changed the way a lot of people lived—and *where* they lived. Most new businesses in the United States during this period were located in cities—especially cities in the northern part of the country. (The South was still recovering from the Civil War and wouldn't catch up to the North for many years.) The kind of business you'd find depended on where you looked. Some areas of the country saw increases in coal mining, while others saw big jumps in the manufacture of clothing, automobiles, goods made of steel, and industrial machinery.

As these new businesses grew, they provided many job opportunities. People who had grown tired of trying to scratch out a living as farmers left the rural parts of the nation and moved to the cities, which grew very rapidly as a result. Many new cities were started during this time.

America's industrial production grew at an astonishing rate between the Civil War and the first two decades of the twentieth century. But while many Americans became very rich during this time, many more still lived in miserable poverty. They may have had jobs and a fairly steady income, but most made barely enough to survive.

Many workers were unhappy with their pay and with their working conditions. That led to the formation of labor unions in the United

HISTORY MAKERS

Samuel Gompers (1850–1924) was an important figure in the history of American labor unions, groups of workers who band together to demand better pay and job conditions from their employers. Gompers, who was born in England, founded the American Federation of Labor (AFL), a collection of labor unions in the United States. He served as the AFL's president from 1886 until 1894 and from 1895 until his death in 1924.

States, starting in 1869. Unions were formed when all the workers in a factory joined together to bargain with the business owners for higher pay and better working conditions. At first, the growth of this new labor movement was slow, but after the turn of the century, more and more workers joined labor unions.

Even though there were many problems to overcome—including some serious slowdowns in the US economy—America enjoyed a time of rapid economic expansion during the nineteenth and early twentieth centuries. The nation grew not only as an economic force but also as a military power. During the second decade of the twentieth century, that would prove to be very important, not only to the United States but to the rest of the world as well.

The World Goes to War

World history is filled with all kinds of wars between individual nations. But World War I was the first war fought between countries from all around the globe. World War I started in 1914 in Europe, but the United States didn't get involved until 1917.

World War I started over the assassination of two people: Austria's Archduke Franz Ferdinand and his wife, Sophie. On June 28, 1914, a Serbian man named Gavrilo Princip shot and killed the archduke and duchess while they visited the city of Sarajevo in the Austro-Hungarian province of Bosnia-Herzegovina.

Archduke Ferdinand was the nephew of Austria's emperor and was in line to become emperor after his uncle, but he was not very well liked in his country. At that time, Austria-Hungary (a union between Austria and Hungary that began in 1867) had been having problems with Serbia, and Ferdinand's assassination gave Austria-Hungary a good reason to attack.

Before attacking, though, Austria-Hungary made sure it had the backing of Germany, which had a treaty with Austria-Hungary. In the time between Archduke Ferdinand's assassination and the actual attack, Serbia gained the support of Russia, with whom the Serbians had a treaty. Russia also had treaties with France and Britain, which brought them both into the conflict.

Austria-Hungary officially declared war on Serbia on July 28, 1914. On August 1, Germany declared war on Russia, and two days later also declared war on France. On August 4, Britain declared war on Germany after the Germans invaded Belgium. Then, on August 6, Austria-Hungary declared war on Russia and Serbia declared war on Germany.

So at the start of World War I, three nations—France, Great Britain, and Russia—formed what was called the Entente Powers (or the Allies). Later, several other countries joined the Allies' fight against the Central Powers of Germany and Austria-Hungary.

The United States Enters World War I

The Entente Powers wanted the United States to join the war against the Central Powers. By 1917, after two years of fighting under terrible conditions, the Allies were running out of young men and supplies to fight the war. They knew America had a lot of soldiers, weapons, and supplies, and they did everything they could to persuade the United States to help them.

At that time, however, US foreign policy was based on "isolationism," which meant America would not get involved in other countries' wars. Many American leaders and citizens believed that the United States should not fight in a war that was so far away and didn't directly affect America.

But two major international events involving Germany and the United States helped bring the United States into World War I. First, on May 7, 1915, a German U-boat (submarine) fired torpedoes at the British ocean liner RMS *Lusitania*. The ship sank in 18 minutes, and 1,198 of the 1,959 people aboard died—including 159 Americans. The sinking of the *Lusitania* made most Americans very angry, and it soon became a symbol used in military recruiting campaigns.

The second incident was an intercepted message between Germany and Mexico early in 1917, called the Zimmermann Telegram. In the telegram, German foreign secretary Arthur Zimmermann promised Mexico help in reclaiming territories it had lost in the Mexican-American War if the United States entered World War I and sided with the Allies. The Germans hoped that a war between the United States and Mexico would keep the Americans occupied with fighting on their own soil. The British intercepted the message and warned the United States of its contents.

When the press revealed the contents of the Zimmermann Telegram, the American public became angry at the Germans. This time, they were ready to go to war because the Germans had attempted to stir up a war between the United States and Mexico.

On April 2, 1917, President Woodrow Wilson asked Congress for a formal declaration of war against Germany. Congress granted the request four days later, meaning that the United States was now officially at war with Germany. General John J. Pershing was put in command of US forces in Europe. On June 26, 1917, the first American troops landed in St. Nazaire, France.

Russia Gets Out

As the United States entered World War I, internal conflict in Russia was about to lead to that nation's withdrawal from the war. In 1917 Czar Nicholas II was removed from power largely because he had led Russia into World War I, which led to the deaths of millions of Russians and left the nation in ruins. The new Russian government wanted out of the war so it could focus on rebuilding. On March 3, 1918, Russia signed the Brest-Litovsk Treaty with Germany, which ended Russia's involvement in World War I.

Russia's withdrawal from the war meant Germany could move troops that had been fighting on the eastern front in Russia back to the west, where they could face the American soldiers. Millions of soldiers and civilians died during the following year, but the Americans' entry into the war began turning the war in the Allies' favor.

European troops had been fighting and dying for more than three years, and the ones who remained were exhausted. The American soldiers were fresher and ready to continue the fight. It wasn't long before the Allies began advancing against the Central Powers.

On November 11, 1918, Germany surrendered and signed an agreement, called the Armistice, at Compiègne, France. The Armistice called for the fighting to end at the eleventh hour of the eleventh day of the eleventh month—11:00 in the morning on November 11. World War I was finally over—and not a moment too soon for many European nations. By the time the fighting stopped, about 10 million soldiers had died—an average of 6,500 for every day of the war—in addition to millions of civilians.

The Treaty of Versailles

On January 18, 1919, diplomats from several of the countries involved in World War I met at a peace conference in Versailles, France, to draft an agreement (or treaty) that would result in the official end of World War I. That agreement was called the Treaty of Versailles, which representatives from Germany and the Allied Powers signed on June 28, 1919.

The Treaty of Versailles was meant not just to end the war in Europe but to punish Germany for its part in the conflict. The treaty stated that the Germans would

1. take full responsibility for the damage caused during World War I (this is known as the "war guilt" clause)
2. give up much of its land (including its overseas colonies)
3. have its army limited to 100,000 soldiers
4. pay large amounts of money to the Allied Powers.

iNTERESTiNG!

The three most important and influential men at the Paris Peace Conference in 1919 were British Prime Minister David Lloyd George, French Prime Minister Georges Clemenceau, and US President Woodrow Wilson. Germany was not represented at the conference.

On May 7, 1919, the Treaty of Versailles—which the Germans were told to sign within three weeks, or else!—was sent to the Germans. Because the treaty was so harsh on the Germans, they sent back a list of complaints about the agreement. The Allies ignored most of those complaints.

Rather than sign the Treaty of Versailles, German chancellor Philipp Scheidemann resigned. But the Germans had no military power to resist, so they had no choice but to sign the treaty. On June 28, 1919—five years to the day after the assassination of Archduke Franz Ferdinand—German representatives Hermann Müller and Johannes Bell signed the Versailles Treaty.

World War I had ended, but that was not the last time Germany would play a major role in starting a worldwide war. Many historians believe that the terms and conditions of the Treaty of Versailles punished the Germans so harshly that it helped create the conditions for the rise of the Nazis in Germany and the outbreak of World War II.

CHAPTER 7

America Becomes a World Power

World War II through the Korean War

From the 1860s through the end of World War I, the United States enjoyed an amazing time of prosperity. Sure, there were some downturns along the way, but for the most part, nearly all parts of the American economy—especially manufacturing—boomed during this period.

After its success in World War I, the US military had a reputation as a strong power. After the war ended, the United States enjoyed a decade of economic growth and peace that are now called the Roaring Twenties.

Many people thought the peace and prosperity of the 1920s would never end. But starting in 1929, the United States (and the rest of the world) went through the difficult times you'll read about in this chapter: the Great Depression and World War II.

In this chapter, you'll also read about how world politics and military power changed by the end of World War II. You'll see how the United States and the Soviet Union, or USSR, became the two world military powers and how they entered into a decades-long rivalry that would change the world even more.

The Great Depression

During the 1930s, the United States went through a very difficult time called the Great Depression. This period in United States history began in September 1929, when the US stock market fell very quickly, causing many people to lose money they had invested in companies and corporations. Then on October 29, a day that came to be known as Black Tuesday, the stock markets suffered a second straight day of huge losses, costing thousands of investors many millions of dollars. Some people lost everything they had! The stock market crash scared many Americans and caused them to start saving their money rather than spending it. Because people

stopped spending, countless banks, businesses, and factories went out of business, which caused millions of people to lose their jobs and the money they had saved. Many of those people ended up homeless and penniless.

During the worst part of the Great Depression, the unemployment rate in the United States—meaning the percentage of people who wanted to work but couldn't find a job—was over 25 percent. Many of these people had to depend on the government or on private charities just to have a place to stay and enough food to eat.

The Great Depression didn't affect just the United States. It hurt almost every country in the world, and many nations had it worse than the United States. During the Great Depression, international trade dropped by about 50 percent. That's partly because countries raised tariffs (taxes on imported and exported goods) in an effort to protect their own businesses and industries. In some countries, the unemployment rate reached as high as 33 percent—one out of every three people was out of work.

FDR's "New Deal"

Herbert Hoover was president of the United States at the start of the Great Depression. After the October 1929 stock market crash, the US economy got worse almost every day. More and more people lost their jobs and their homes.

In 1932 Franklin Roosevelt was elected president, and almost immediately he began taking steps that he—and the rest of the nation—hoped would bring the country out of the Great Depression. Together, these steps were called the New Deal.

President Roosevelt's "New Deal" of 1934–1936 included many government programs that gave jobs to people who were out of work. For example, the Civilian Conservation Corps (CCC) put many young men to work in national forests. Also the Works Progress Administration (WPA) created many different types of jobs, including jobs in road, public school, and airport construction. Probably the best-known New Deal project was the Tennessee Valley Authority (TVA), which resulted in the construction of dams and electrical power plants along the Tennessee River.

The New Deal was also the beginning of Social Security, which is a government-run system that provides income for retired workers or those who can no longer work because they are sick or injured.

The New Deal included government programs that were meant to keep people from losing all their money if their bank went out of business. One of those programs created the Federal Deposit Insurance Corporation (FDIC), which replaces people's lost money when a bank either loses money or has to close its doors. Having the FDIC in place to insure against the loss of cash helped people begin to trust banks again.

A Slow and Painful Recovery

Different countries started to recover from the Great Depression at different times. For most, the recovery started in 1933. The United States' recovery began in the spring of 1933, but it was slow going for several more years. By 1940 the unemployment rate in the United States was down to 15 percent—better than the 25 percent during the worst part of the Depression, but still very high.

Over the past several decades, historians and economists (people who specialize in the study of the world's economies) have argued about what brought about the end of the Great Depression. Some believe the end came as a result of President Roosevelt's New Deal, while others believe military spending on World War II played a much more important role in bringing the United States out of its worst-ever economic downturn. Many others believe it was a combination of both.

WORTH REPEATING

"The only thing we have to fear is fear itself."
—President Franklin Roosevelt, during his first inaugural address in 1933

DID YOU KNOW?

The New Deal described in this chapter was actually President Roosevelt's second recovery plan. The first, which was put into effect in 1933–1934, set price and wage controls in all industries and also cut farm production to raise prices of goods produced on farms. This first New Deal ended in March 1935, when the US Supreme Court declared it unconstitutional.

THE ALLIED NATIONS
VS. THE AXIS POWERS

Allied Nations
The British Empire
The Soviet Union (Russia)
The United States
France
Poland
China
Australia
Belgium
Brazil
Canada
Czechoslovakia
Ethiopia
Greece
Mexico
The Netherlands
New Zealand
Norway
Union of South Africa
Yugoslavia

Axis Nations
Germany
Japan
Italy
Hungary
Romania
Bulgaria
Finland*
Iraq*
Thailand*
San Marino*
Yugoslavia*
India*
*Nations that did not sign an official pact with the Axis nations but were allied with them during World War II.

There is no question, though, that the Great Depression ended at about the same time nations of the world began spending massive amounts of money on war materials at the start of World War II. It's also true that this increased spending provided jobs for people who had been unemployed.

World War II: How It All Started

World War II began in 1939 and ended in 1945. It was the most widespread military conflict in human history. Almost every nation in the world was involved, and eventually two opposing sides developed: the Allies, which included the United States, Great Britain, and the Soviet Union (Russia), also known as The Big Three; and the Axis, which included Germany, Italy, and Japan.

Even though World War II started in 1939, the United States didn't get involved until 1941. The American military fought World War II on two different fronts or "theaters"—one in the Pacific Ocean against Japan, and the other against the Axis powers in Europe. Before the war ended in 1945, more than 400,000 Americans lost their lives. A total of more than 72 million people—mostly civilians—died in World War II.

In some very important ways, the effects of the Great Depression led the world into World War II. Many of the nations worst affected by the Great Depression changed their leaders and their forms of government during that time. That included Germany, where Adolf Hitler's Nazi party rose to power and took control in January 1933.

The war in the Pacific started on July 7, 1937, when Japan invaded China. Earlier, the Japanese had invaded Manchuria, where they began developing industries and mining, believing it would stimulate economic growth and help bring Japan out of the Great Depression.

The European war began on September 1, 1939, when the Nazis began their invasion of Poland. Hitler wanted to expand his empire throughout Europe, including what was then the Soviet Union. He thought the best way to do that was to first invade Poland, which had been given some German territory after World War I.

War Spreads through Europe

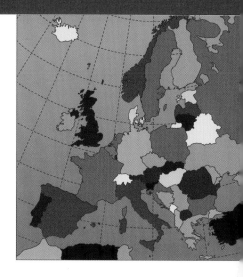

After Germany invaded Poland, Britain and France quickly declared war on the Nazis. Germany easily overran Poland, and then in the spring of 1940, the Germans conquered Norway and Denmark. They followed those conquests by taking the Netherlands (also known as Holland), Belgium, and then France.

By then Germany controlled all of western Europe except for Great Britain. Hitler wanted to take Britain, too, so he started bombing the nation for weeks at a time in hopes the British people would be weakened enough for another easy German invasion.

The Germans bombed Britain all through the summer of 1940. The British fought back valiantly, shooting down large numbers of German planes. In October 1940, Hitler abandoned his plans to invade Britain and turned his attention to the Soviet Union, which he invaded in June 1941.

The United States supported Great Britain during this time, sending money, weapons, and ships. The United States had declared neutrality in the war, meaning the Americans would stay out of the conflict. But after German submarines sank several American ships, the United States moved closer to war with the Axis powers.

> **INTERESTING!**
>
> One of the reasons Nazi Germany was so successful early in World War II—at least until the United States joined the Allies—was a military strategy called blitzkrieg, which means "lightning war." This strategy called for tanks, planes, and soldiers to attack all at the same time. Using this strategy, Germany overwhelmed the smaller armies of its neighbors.

December 7, 1941: When World War II Became America's War

During the first few years of World War II, the American public was reluctant to get involved in the conflict. World War I was still fresh in most Americans' minds, and they didn't want to enter another war that could cost many thousands of American lives. That changed on December 7, 1941. At 7:55 that morning, the first wave of Japanese planes attacked the American naval base at Pearl Harbor in Oahu, Hawaii.

With little chance to prepare, American ships and sailors were nearly defenseless as the first wave of 183 Japanese warplanes attacked, followed by a second wave of 167 planes an hour later. The Americans tried to fight back, but by the time the attack was over, 21 of the 96 ships anchored in Pearl Harbor had been sunk,

HISTORIC
HAPPENINGS

HISTORIC HAPPENINGS

Eight US Navy battleships, three destroyers, and four other smaller ships were damaged in the December 7, 1941, attack on Pearl Harbor. Among the battleship casualties:

USS *Arizona,* which sank nine minutes after being struck by a torpedo, killing 1,177 aboard.

USS *Oklahoma,* which rolled on its side and pinned many of its crew underwater inside the ship. Of the Oklahoma's crew of 1,301, 429 died.

USS *West Virginia* sank after being struck numerous times by both torpedoes and bombs.

USS *Nevada,* after being struck several times by torpedoes and bombs during the first attack wave, the *Nevada* tried to get out to sea through the narrow channel leading into the harbor. Planes in the second wave attempted to sink the *Nevada* and block the channel, but the *Nevada*'s crew chose to run the ship aground instead.

WORTH REPEATING

"I fear that we have awakened a sleeping giant and filled him with a terrible resolve."
—Japanese Admiral Isoroku Yamamoto, after the attack on Pearl Harbor

and others had been badly damaged. The Japanese also attacked Hickam, Wheeler, and Bellows airfields, destroying 188 planes and damaging 159 more. A total of 2,403 people, including 68 civilians, died in the attack, and 1,178 more were wounded.

The day after the attack, President Roosevelt asked the United States Congress to declare war on Japan. Not only did Congress answer with an overwhelming "Yes!" but the American public was now united in a common goal: Make the Japanese pay for their attack on Pearl Harbor.

But the United States wouldn't be going to war only with Japan. On December 11, 1941, Germany and Italy declared war on the United States, which meant American forces would be fighting in the European theater of World War II and not just in the Pacific.

The Turning Point in the Pacific War

Within a week of the Pearl Harbor attack, Japan invaded the Philippines, Burma, and Hong Kong. Later, the Japanese also took Borneo, Java, and Sumatra. It was starting to look as if the Japanese had an overwhelming advantage against the United States. But things began to turn against Japan at the Battle of Midway, which took place June 4–7, 1942 (about six months after Pearl Harbor) at Midway Atoll—about one-third of the way across the Pacific Ocean between Honolulu, Hawaii, and Tokyo, Japan.

By the time the Battle of Midway was over, more than 3,000 Japanese had died and four Japanese aircraft carriers had been destroyed. This was the turning point in the Pacific War. The Allies now had the upper hand, and they used it to launch a huge counteroffensive (a time of fighting back) against the Japanese.

The US Navy, under the command of Admiral Chester Nimitz, launched the first stage of the counteroffensive. US Marines landed on the southwest Pacific island of Guadalcanal and other nearby islands in the Solomon Islands. Meanwhile, the US Army, under the command of General Douglas MacArthur and with help from Australian allies, took New Guinea's Papuan peninsula.

Over the next several months, Allied forces, under the command of Nimitz and MacArthur, so weakened the enemy's capabilities that it was only a matter of time before Japan would be completely defeated. In late November 1944, the Allies began strategically bombing the islands of Japan.

Even though there were two major campaigns left in the Pacific War—on Luzon in the Philippines and at Okinawa, Japan—the Japanese naval forces had been beaten down to the point that they were defenseless. Japan's air force had also been virtually destroyed. Not only that, Japanese cities were being bombed almost daily.

Victory in Europe

At first, the war in Europe didn't go very well for the United States and the rest of the Allied forces. Germany and the Axis won decisive victories everywhere they went. All through 1942, Germany continued bombing British cities. That summer, the Germans marched through southern Russia toward a huge city called Stalingrad (now Volgograd). The Nazis also had control of North Africa.

But the war began to turn the Allies' way in 1943. The Battle of Stalingrad raged on between August 1942 and early February 1943. On February 2, after an estimated two million military and civilian deaths, the Nazis and their allies were forced to surrender. Like the Battle of Midway in the

HISTORY MAKERS

George Smith Patton III (1885–1945) was a US Army officer who is best remembered for his leadership as a commander during World War II. As a US Army general, Patton played a key role in the Allied invasion and victory in North Africa in November 1942. He also led advances across France and Germany in 1944–1945, which led to the end of World War II.

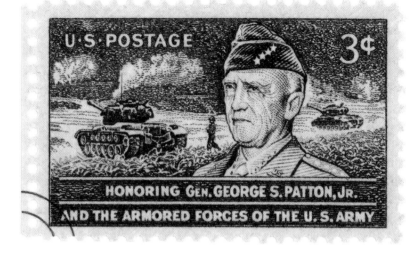

WORTH REPEATING

"You will bring about the destruction of the German war machine, the elimination of Nazi tyranny over the oppressed peoples of Europe, and security for ourselves in a free world. . . . I have full confidence in your courage, devotion to duty, and skill in battle. We will accept nothing less than full victory. Good luck, and let us all beseech the blessings of Almighty God upon this great and noble undertaking."
—General Dwight D. Eisenhower, giving the D-day order on June 6, 1944

Pacific War, the Battle of Stalingrad proved to be a turning point in the European theater.

Later that year, British and American troops took North Africa from the Nazis. Once the Allies had control of North Africa, they turned their attention to Italy. In September 1943, Italian troops officially surrendered to the Allies. Meanwhile, the Soviets were driving the Germans out of one Soviet city after another.

Even though the Allies were making advances all over Europe, Germany wasn't ready to give up the fight. The Nazis fought to keep control of Italy, but Allied forces held on and continued making gains there.

On June 6, 1944, American, British, and Canadian troops landed on the beaches of Normandy, France. This was called D-day. The Americans suffered many casualties, but the massive invasion ended with the Allies in control of the French beaches, and it was the beginning of the end for Hitler's control of France. Two months later, Paris was liberated. After that, the Allies made steady progress against the Axis powers all over Europe as German troops began retreating toward Berlin, the German capital.

In December 1944, the Germans began one last counterattack against the Allies. It was called the Battle of the Bulge, and it took place in parts of Belgium, Luxembourg, and France. At first, the German army was successful, but in January 1945, Hitler had to withdraw his troops.

The Allies were victorious over the Nazis in the Battle of the Bulge, and it was only a matter of months before the Allied victory was complete. In the spring of 1945, Soviet troops attacked Berlin while American and British troops strengthened their hold on Italy. In April 1945, Adolf Hitler killed himself, and in early May the Germans surrendered. The European part of World War II was over.

In the final days of the war, the Allies made a terrible discovery inside Nazi Germany. As the Soviets marched through Eastern Europe and into Germany, they found many concentration camps where the Nazis imprisoned Jews, political prisoners, gypsies, and other people they didn't like. Some of the camps were prisons where people were treated terribly and made to perform slave labor. But some camps were death camps, where people were sent to be murdered. The Nazis murdered millions of people in these camps. This terrible part of human history is called the Holocaust.

INTERESTING!

The Soviet Union was formed in 1922, after the Russian Revolution of 1917, when Russia joined with the Ukraine, Belorussia (now Belarus), the Trancaucasian Federation (Armenia, Azerbaijan, and Georgia) to form the Union of Soviet Socialist Republics (the USSR). By 1940 nine more republics joined the USSR for a total of fifteen. The Soviet Union was dissolved in 1991.

Japan's Final Surrender

On August 6, 1945, a Boeing B-29 bomber called the *Enola Gay* flew over the Japanese city of Hiroshima and dropped the first atomic bomb ever used during wartime. The bomb, which was code-named Little Boy, caused massive destruction and the deaths of tens of thousands of people. Three days later, a second atomic bomb fell—this one code-named Fat Man—this time on the city of Nagasaki.

Some important military figures from the United States were sure that dropping two atomic bombs on Japan—only a few days apart—would quickly cause the Japanese to surrender. That is exactly what happened.

Over the decades since the United States dropped two atomic bombs on Japan, ending the war in the Pacific, people have argued and debated whether or not it was the right thing to do. People who believe it was right say that dropping the bombs meant Allied forces would not have to invade mainland Japan, meaning many Allied lives would be saved. But people who oppose the use of the atomic weapons argue that the United States was going to win the war anyway, so there was no reason to use weapons that caused such terrible death and destruction.

On August 15, 1945, Japanese Emperor Hirohito announced his country's surrender and ordered his soldiers to stop fighting. On September 2, officials from the Japanese government boarded the USS *Missouri* and signed the Japanese surrender. The war in Europe had already ended by this time, meaning that September 2, 1945 (now known as V-J Day—for "Victory over Japan") marked the end of the biggest, bloodiest war in human history.

A New Kind of War—The Cold War

When World War II ended, the world looked very different from how it had been before the war. Most important, Germany, Japan, and Italy were no longer the military powers they had once been. Now, only two world powers—the United States and the Soviet Union—were left.

The United States and the Soviet Union had been allies against Nazi Germany and the rest of the Axis countries during World War II, but not long after the war ended, the two countries entered into a long period of mutual distrust—and ill will—toward each other. This period of history is known as the Cold War.

During the Cold War, which began in about 1947 and ended in 1991, the United States and the USSR engaged in political conflict, military threats, and proxy wars (meaning wars fought by or for countries allied with either the United States or the USSR) between what was called the "Communist world" (the Soviet Union and its allies) and the "Western world" (the United States and its allies).

During the Cold War, the United States and the USSR never entered into any direct major military conflict with each other. But the two countries were fierce rivals in just about every other way imaginable. Both nations placed military forces in strategic parts of the world, and each spied on the other and spread propaganda. They both spent billions of dollars on an "arms race," with both countries stockpiling nuclear and conventional weapons.

America's First Real "Cold War" War

The Korean War, which started on June 25, 1950, and ended on July 27, 1953, was the first major armed conflict between the Communist world and the non-Communist world. It started when Communist North Korea invaded non-Communist South Korea. Although the Soviet Union stayed out of the war for the most part, armed forces from the United States and China fought in the war.

Japan ruled the Korean Peninsula starting in 1910 and ending with its defeat in World War II. Following Japan's surrender in 1945, the peninsula was divided along the Thirty-eighth Parallel (a line going all the way around the earth 38 degrees north of the equator). After World War II, troops from the United States occupied the southern part of the peninsula and troops from the Soviet Union occupied the North. In 1948 the South and the North established separate governments. The Communist North was called the Democratic People's Republic of Korea, and the South was called the Republic of Korea.

There had been minor battles and raids between the two sides in the months leading up to the invasion, but all-out war started between North Korea and South Korea on June 25, 1950, when the North Korean army crossed the Thirty-eighth Parallel—the border between the two countries—and invaded its neighbor to the south.

After the invasion, US President Harry Truman felt a lot of public pressure to do something about it. This was during the Cold War, and most people in the United States saw Communism as the world's biggest threat. Truman met with his advisers, who recommended that the US military conduct air strikes against North Korean targets. Truman ordered the air strikes and also ordered the US Navy's Seventh Fleet to move into position to protect the island of Formosa (now Taiwan).

Going to War...But Not Alone

HISTORY MAKERS

Douglas MacArthur (1880–1964) not only served as the UN's supreme commander during the first part of the Korean War, he also served as supreme commander of the Allied war effort in the Pacific during World War II. MacArthur also directed the Allies' postwar occupation of Japan. Early in the Korean War, he planned the landing at Inchon, which helped South Korea take back territory North Korea had taken when it invaded in 1950. MacArthur retired from military service as the most decorated serviceman in American history.

On June 25, 1950, the United Nations Security Council unanimously passed Resolution 82, which condemned the invasion of South Korea. The Soviet Union, which had veto power over UN Security Council resolutions, boycotted the meeting. Two days later, the Security Council published Resolution 83, which recommended that member nations offer military assistance to South Korea.

North Korea had a lot more soldiers than South Korea, though the South's troops were better trained and had better equipment. Not only that, the suddenness of the attack surprised the South. North Korea would likely have overrun South Korea had it not been for help from the United States and the UN.

At first, the Korean War didn't go very well for the United States and its allies. Early on, North Korean soldiers overwhelmed the UN forces and drove them into a small area around the city of Pusan, which is located in the southeastern corner of the Korean Peninsula. The forces desperately held their position along what was called the Pusan Perimeter.

President Harry S. Truman

US general Douglas MacArthur, the UN supreme commander in Korea, knew something had to be done before it was too late. He wanted to order an invasion far behind the North Korean troops at Inchon, which was on the peninsula's west coast. After receiving approval for the attack, MacArthur ordered the invasion. On September 15, 1950, the first UN troops stormed the beach at Inchon.

The attack caught North Korea completely by surprise. The UN forces quickly took Inchon and then marched toward Seoul, the capital city of South Korea, which the North Koreans had captured earlier. On September 25, after days of terrible fighting, the UN forces retook Seoul. Meanwhile, forces that had been trapped at the Pusan Perimeter were able to break out and push the enemy toward the north.

After the landing at Inchon and the breakout from the Pusan Perimeter, the North Koreans were in full retreat. UN forces quickly retook all of South Korea and continued north, into North Korea. It looked like the war was almost over.

A Whole New Problem in Korea

After UN troops reached the Yalu River on the border of North Korea and Communist China, the Chinese feared that they were about to be invaded. In late November 1950, Chinese soldiers poured into North Korea. Now the UN and South Korea were fighting two enemies: North Korea and China.

China's attack pushed the UN troops back to the Thirty-eighth Parallel, the original border between North and South Korea. The key battle in China's offensive was called the Battle of Chosin Reservoir, which resulted in a major loss for the UN forces. The United States First Marine Division suffered the heaviest losses in the battle.

General MacArthur urged President Truman to declare war on China, and even wanted the United States to use atomic weapons against the Chinese. When he openly criticized President Truman in 1951, he was relieved of his command.

The Korean War continued on into 1953, with neither side taking much territory from the other. When Dwight D. Eisenhower became the thirty-fourth president of the United States, he decided to end the war, which he called a "stalemate," meaning neither side could win. That made the Korean War the first war the United States fought in and did not win.

During much of the war, officials from both sides took part in talks to bring peace back to the Korean Peninsula. That peace came on July 27, 1953, when representatives from North Korea, China, and the UN signed a cease-fire called the Korean Armistice Agreement. The agreement established a demilitarized zone (DMZ) around the Thirty-eighth Parallel. To this day, troops from North Korea on one side and South Korea and the United States on the other defend the DMZ.

Even though more than four million people died in the Korean War, including more than 50,000 Americans, the Korean War isn't as well remembered as either World War II or the Vietnam War. That is why the Korean War is often called "America's Forgotten War." ❌

CHAPTER 8

Four Decades of Big Change

The 1960s through Y2K

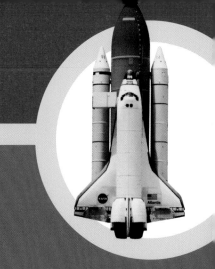

One thing you've probably noticed as you've read through this book is that US history is filled with all kinds of changes—changes in how people live, think, and do business with one another.

But in the period of American history between the end of the 1950s through the close of the twentieth century, it seemed as if everything that *could* change *did* change. The world underwent huge changes in technology and business, and the culture in the United States was almost completely transformed.

Even though good things happened during the 1960s (for example, the US government passed civil rights legislation that gave African Americans the same rights as everyone else), the United States went through sometimes painful social change, due in large part to the Vietnam War.

During this era, the United States also became the world's only military superpower when the Soviet Union broke apart in the early 1990s. That event changed the already large role the United States played throughout the world.

This chapter will give you a quick look at the events that took place between 1960 and the end of the millennium. After you've read it, you'll understand how different the world became in just 40 years.

When the "Cold War" Heated Up

One of the most important—and scary—Cold War events was what is now called the Cuban Missile Crisis, which took place in 1962. The Cuban Missile Crisis is regarded as the closest the world has ever come to widespread nuclear war.

The Cuban Missile Crisis involved three countries: the United States, the Soviet Union, and of course, Cuba. The crisis came to national attention on October 14, 1962, when a US Air Force U-2 spy plane captured pictures

113

HISTORIC HAPPENINGS

On April 16, 1961, less than three months after John F. Kennedy was sworn in as president of the United States, a military force made up of Cuban exiles who had been trained by the Central Intelligence Agency (CIA) attempted to overthrow the government of Cuban dictator Fidel Castro when they launched what is now known as the Bay of Pigs Invasion. The exiles, who had the support and encouragement of the US government, were defeated in less than three days by Cuban armed forces, which had been trained and equipped by the Soviet Union.

WORTH REPEATING

"We will not prematurely or unnecessarily risk the costs of worldwide nuclear war in which even the fruits of victory would be ashes in our mouth—but neither will we shrink from that risk at any time it must be faced."
—President John F. Kennedy, in an October 22, 1962, speech to the nation

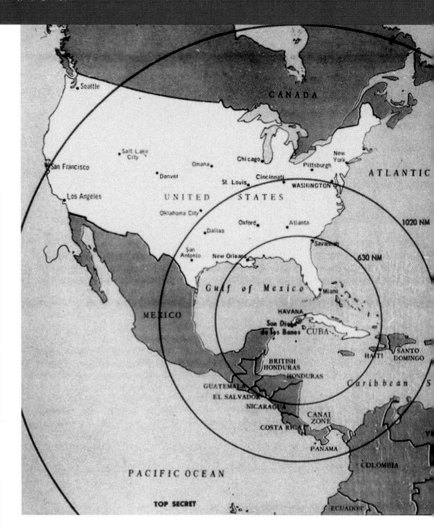

proving that the Soviet Union was constructing missile bases in Cuba, which is located only 90 miles from the Florida coast.

Cuba and the Soviet Union began construction of the bases, which would have housed missiles with the ability to strike most of the continental United States, after unsuccessful attempts by the United States to overthrow Fidel Castro's Cuban regime in 1961. Also, in 1958 the United States had installed nuclear-tipped missiles in Italy and Turkey, and the Soviets wanted to have their own weapons closer to North America.

When President Kennedy announced the situation to the American public, he said the United States had demanded that the Soviets dismantle

the missile bases under construction in Cuba and remove all their offensive weapons. He also announced that the United States would impose a blockade around Cuba, not allowing any ships to sail to Cuba. The United States also considered military attack on Cuba.

Kennedy's administration didn't believe the Soviets would agree to his demands, but thought they were prepared for a military conflict with the United States. In a letter to President Kennedy, Soviet leader Nikita Khrushchev said that the announced blockade of Cuba was "an act of aggression propelling humankind into the abyss of a world nuclear-missile war."

The confrontation ended peacefully—and quickly. On October 28, 1962, President Kennedy and the United Nations secretary-general reached an agreement with the Soviet Union. The Soviets agreed they would close their weapons bases in Cuba in exchange for an American promise never to invade Cuba again. In a secret agreement, the United States also agreed to remove some of its weapons systems from Europe and Turkey.

Entering the Vietnam War... One Step at a Time

The second of the United States' wars fought during the Cold War period was the Vietnam War. Vietnam is a small country in Southeast Asia. The Vietnam War, which began in 1957 and ended in 1975, was fought between Communist North Vietnam and non-Communist South Vietnam.

During the Vietnam War, the Soviet Union, China, and North Korea supported North Vietnam, while the United States—along with allies Thailand, Australia, New Zealand, and the Philippines—supported South Vietnam. The Soviet Union never sent fighting troops to the Vietnam War, but the United States did.

The war happened because North Vietnam wanted to reunite North and South into a single nation. The two countries were separated in 1954, after France was defeated in a conflict called the First Indochina War. For many years before that, the country was called French Indochina.

After the First Indochina War, the plan was for French Indochina to temporarily split into two countries until closely supervised free elections could be held in 1956. The elections were never held, so the two remained split—into the Democratic Republic of Vietnam (the North) and the State of Vietnam (the South).

Starting around 1957, a group called the Vietcong, which called itself the National Liberation Front (NLF), began assassinating important people in South Vietnam. The Vietcong were actually South Vietnamese rebels who agreed with North Vietnam's goal of uniting the North and South into one country.

Before sending troops to fight in Vietnam, the United States backed the anti-Communist government in South Vietnam. That included sending military advisers to help train the South Vietnamese army. In

1959 North Vietnam started giving more and more military assistance to the Vietcong, which used that assistance in attacks on South Vietnamese military units. The United States responded to these attacks by sending even more help to South Vietnam, including soldiers who served as military advisers.

A Terrible Day for the United States

As the 1964 presidential election approached, President Kennedy was confident he would easily defeat his Republican opponent, Arizona Senator Barry Goldwater. Kennedy believed a big win would mean he had the support of the American people for the changes he wanted to make in the country. But he also knew there would still be some roadblocks to his plan. In Texas, Vice President Lyndon Johnson's home state, a disagreement between Governor John Connally and Senator Ralph Yarborough prompted President Kennedy to tour the state of Texas with both men to give the public a show of unity in the party.

HISTORY MAKERS

Barry Goldwater (1909–1998) was a conservative politician who represented the state of Arizona for five terms in the US Senate. Goldwater was the Republican Party's nominee for president in the 1964 election, but he lost to Democrat Lyndon Johnson. Goldwater was known as "Mr. Conservative" because he helped lead a resurgence of the conservative movement in the United States in the 1960s.

HISTORIC HAPPENINGS

On July 2, 1964, President Lyndon Johnson signed the Civil Rights Act of 1964, which outlawed many forms of discrimination against African Americans and women. This legislation, which passed Congress despite objections from many Southern Democrats, was intended to address some of the problems that arose after Reconstruction. It ended voter registration requirements designed to keep blacks from voting, as well as racial segregation in schools, at the workplace, and at facilities that served the general public.

On Friday, November 22, 1963, President Kennedy and his wife, Jacqueline, were riding in an open limousine traveling in a motorcade through downtown Dallas. Governor Connally was riding with them, and the three waved at crowds gathered on the streets to see the president.

At 12:30 in the afternoon, shots rang out, and the president was struck in the neck and head. Though he was rushed to the hospital, President Kennedy died a few hours later. Governor Connally was also seriously wounded in the attack, but he survived. Vice President Lyndon Johnson took the oath of office as president just minutes after the announcement that Kennedy had died.

Investigators quickly discovered that the shots that killed President Kennedy had come from a sixth-floor window of the Texas School Book Depository building. Lee Harvey Oswald, an employee in the building, was seen leaving the building right after the shots were fired. It wasn't long before police arrested Oswald in a movie theater.

Police questioned Oswald for two days. Oswald claimed he was innocent, but it was discovered that he had purchased the rifle used in the shooting for $12.78 through a mail-order business. Also, his palm prints were found on the rifle.

Once the police were done questioning Oswald, they led him from the Dallas city jail to the county jail. As Oswald was being led out, Jack Ruby, a Dallas nightclub owner with connections to organized crime, shot and killed the accused assassin. Ruby was arrested on the spot and was later convicted of murder for killing Oswald. On January 3, 1967, he died of lung cancer—while awaiting a second trial in the killing of Oswald.

On November 25, 1963, President Kennedy's body was buried at Arlington National Cemetery in Virginia. Representatives from more than 90 nations, including the Soviet Union, attended the funeral. Jacqueline Kennedy lit an "eternal flame," which still burns over President Kennedy's grave.

A New President, a New Policy in Vietnam

Under President Kennedy, US involvement in the Vietnam War was limited to aid and advice to the South Vietnamese military. That changed under President Johnson, who, in 1965, began sending hundreds of thousands of combat troops to Vietnam. By 1968 around a half million US soldiers were serving there.

Starting on January 31, 1968, North Vietnamese soldiers, along with the Vietcong, began a military campaign against South Vietnam and the United States called the Tet Offensive. They attacked military and civilian targets throughout South Vietnam in hopes of winning the war with a massive and focused assault that would lead to the fall of the South Vietnamese government in Saigon.

Up to that point, the Tet Offensive was the largest military operation by either side in the Vietnam War. At first the US and South Vietnamese armies were surprised by the

HISTORIC HAPPENINGS

On April 4, 1968, an escapee from the Missouri State Penitentiary named James Earl Ray shot the great civil rights leader Martin Luther King Jr. as he stood on a second-floor balcony of the Lorraine Motel in Memphis, Tennessee. King later died of his wounds. Many of the people who worked with King called for a peaceful response to the murder, but riots broke out in many US cities.

scope of the attack, but they quickly regained control of the areas under attack and inflicted heavy casualties on the Vietcong and North Vietnamese forces.

Although the Tet Offensive resulted in a military victory for South Vietnam and the United States, it was a psychological victory for the Vietcong and caused President Johnson's administration all kinds of trouble at home. The American people, who had been led to believe that the United States and South Vietnam were winning the war, were shocked by the size of the Communist attack. More and more Americans began telling the US government to bring the American troops home from Vietnam and let the South Vietnamese fight for themselves.

The End of the Vietnam War

INTERESTING!

As the Vietnam War dragged on, President Johnson's popularity as president declined steadily. He had won the election in 1964, and he was eligible to run again. But on March 31, 1968, Johnson concluded a nationally televised speech with this announcement: "I shall not seek, and I will not accept, the nomination of my party for another term as your president."

Though President Johnson knew that South Vietnam and the United States had defeated the Vietcong in the Tet Offensive, the Vietcong won the battle of public opinion. Making things worse for President Johnson was a report in 1968 that US forces had suffered the worst week for casualties in the entire war. During 1968 more than 16,500 American soldiers died in the Vietnam War.

After the Tet Offensive, the United States began to slowly withdraw many of its soldiers from the country while training and equipping the South Vietnamese to continue fighting. This policy was called Vietnamization.

In 1973 the United States pulled almost all its troops out of Vietnam. In January of that year, North and South Vietnam signed a peace treaty in

Paris, and the last American ground troops left Vietnam two months later, leaving only a few as military advisers. Even though the cease-fire had been called, fighting between North and South Vietnam started up again soon after the US soldiers left. Without the United States there to defend South Vietnam, North Vietnam attacked, and on April 30, 1975, the war ended when South Vietnam surrendered to North Vietnam. After that, Vietnam was again a united country.

A Man on the Moon

Before we move on to what happened in the United States after the Vietnam War, let's rewind a bit, back to 1961. On May 25 of that year, President Kennedy addressed Congress and proposed a wild idea: that the United States speed up its space program and set a goal of sending astronauts to the moon by the end of the 1960s.

Kennedy's goal of sending a man to the moon before 1970 was part of what is called the Space Race, which was yet another part of the Cold War. By 1961 the Soviet Union had pulled ahead of the United States in the Space Race. In October 1957, the Soviets sent a satellite called *Sputnik* into orbit, and a month later they sent the first

animal (a dog named Laika) into space. Then in April 1961, the Soviets sent the first human—Yuri Gagarin—into space.

The United States had some catching up to do, and President Kennedy knew it. His goal became reality on the morning of July 16, 1969, when a Saturn V rocket carrying the Apollo 11 mission and its crew of astronauts Neil Armstrong, Edwin "Buzz" Aldrin, and Michael Collins launched from Florida's Kennedy Space Center. Apollo 11 included a command module called *Columbia* and a lunar lander (the vehicle that would actually land on the moon's surface) called the *Eagle.*

Three and a half days after blastoff, Apollo 11 reached the moon's orbit. On July 20, astronauts Armstrong and Aldrin landed the *Eagle* on an area of the moon's surface called the Sea of Tranquillity while Collins stayed behind in the command module taking photographs and conducting scientific experiments. About six and a half hours later, with hundreds of millions of people watching on television worldwide, Armstrong became the first human to set foot on the moon's surface when he stepped out of the *Eagle* and put his left foot down.

Aldrin and Armstrong spent three hours on the moon's surface that day, collecting soil and rock samples and setting up instruments. They also planted an American flag and left a commemorative plaque. Armstrong also spoke the famous words, "That's one small step for man, one giant leap for mankind."

Armstrong and Aldrin spent a total of 21 hours on the moon before lifting off in the *Eagle* to return to the spaceship *Columbia* and the voyage back home. The three-man crew splashed down in the Pacific Ocean on July 24, 1969—eight days after liftoff from the moon.

Over the next few years, American astronauts made five more successful moon landings. The last one took place on December 11, 1972. Another mission to the moon, Apollo 13, launched on April 11, 1970, but the astronauts had to return to earth after an oxygen tank exploded, causing severe damage to the spacecraft's electrical system. All three astronauts— James Lovell, John Swigert, and Fred Haise—returned safely.

Neil Armstrong

President Richard S. Nixon

What's a Watergate?

During the Vietnam War, there were many disagreements among the American public about whether the United States should be fighting in such a faraway place. Once the war was over, Americans hoped that their country could start moving in a better direction. But people's optimism started to fade after what is called the Watergate scandal—which began on June 17, 1972, when Washington, DC, police arrested five men for breaking in to the Democratic National Committee headquarters at the Watergate building in Washington.

At first, President Nixon denied any involvement in the burglary. But over a span of several months, more and more evidence mounted against some of Nixon's staff members. Some of the people who had worked for Nixon revealed that the president had recorded several conversations about the break-in, including the fact that he had tried to cover up the scandal.

President Nixon tried to keep the recordings from going public, and after several months of legal battles, the United States Supreme Court ruled that he had to hand over the recordings. President Nixon knew he had two choices: stay in office and face impeachment by the House of Representatives or resign. On August 9, 1974, President Nixon, the thirty-seventh president of the United States, became the first and only president to resign from the highest office in America.

After Nixon's resignation, his vice president, Gerald Ford, took office as the thirty-eighth president of the United States. President Ford later pardoned Nixon, meaning the former president wouldn't have to face criminal charges for his part in the Watergate scandal.

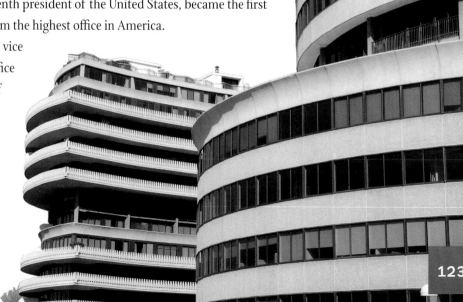

A Tough Four Years

On November 2, 1976, Jimmy Carter, the former governor of Georgia, defeated Gerald Ford to become the thirty-ninth president of the United States. The American people wanted more than anything to put the Watergate scandal behind them, and many hoped that would happen after Carter defeated Ford.

Unfortunately, Carter's presidency was a tough four years for the nation. The national economy suffered due to high inflation, high interest rates, high unemployment, and a severe shortage of oil due to lower sales by oil-producing nations.

But things got a lot worse for President Carter on November 4, 1979, when students in the Middle Eastern nation of Iran stormed the US Embassy in Tehran, the capital city, and took 66 Americans hostage. The students did that in support of what is called the Iranian Revolution (or the Islamic Revolution), which led to the replacement of Iran's monarchy (a system of government with a king) with an Islamic Republic under the rule of Ayatollah Ruholla Khomeini, who led the revolution.

A crowd of about 500 students rushed the embassy after learning that Shah Mohammad Reza Pahlavi, their former national leader (*shah* was an Iranian title for a king), had been admitted to an American hospital for medical treatment. The militants took 66 Americans captive. Of those, 13 were released on November 19 and 20, 1979, and another was released on July 11, 1980. The remaining 52 remained in Iranian captivity.

This incident is called the Iran Hostage Crisis, and it lasted for a total of 444 days. President Carter, who already faced a very difficult reelection campaign because the United States was in the middle of a deep recession, tried everything he could to get the hostages released, but nothing he tried worked.

In 1980 two things happened that helped end the hostage crisis. First, the Shah died in Egypt. Second, Iraq invaded Iran, starting the long and bloody Iran-Iraq War. Now, the Iranians were open to ways to end the hostage crisis. After Ronald Reagan defeated Jimmy Carter in the 1980 presidential election, negotiations for the hostages' release began. Iran released the 52 hostages on January 20, 1981, just as Reagan was completing his inaugural address after being sworn in as the fortieth president of the United States.

HISTORIC HAPPENINGS

Sports fans—and even those who weren't sports fans—from the United States took great pride and satisfaction in a Cold War-era victory over the Soviet Union's hockey team in the 1980 Winter Olympic games in Lake Placid, New York. The Soviets were thought to be unbeatable, but Team USA pulled off one of the greatest upsets in sports history with a 4–3 win. Team USA went on to win the gold medal with a win over Finland in the championship game.

INTERESTING!

In 1980 the United States didn't send athletes to the Summer Olympics, which were held in Moscow, the capital of the Soviet Union. President Carter decided to boycott the Olympics after the Soviet Union invaded Afghanistan in 1979. It was the only time since the modern Olympics began in 1896 that the United States has not participated in an Olympic competition.

The "Reagan Revolution" and the End of the Cold War

Ronald Reagan served as the president of the United States from 1981 until 1989. During that time, he worked to bring the American economy out of a deep recession, to strengthen the US military, and to oppose the Soviet Union wherever he could. The changes President Reagan made are often called the Reagan Revolution.

By the time President Reagan took office in 1981, the Cold War had been going on for more than three decades and had cost the United States *trillions* of dollars and more than 100,000 lives in the Korea and Vietnam wars.

The president saw the Soviet Union as a constant threat to freedom around the world, so he put into action what became known as the Reagan Doctrine. Under the Reagan Doctrine, the United States provided

HISTORIC HAPPENINGS

On Tuesday, January 28, 1986, the people of the United States—including hundreds of thousands viewing on television—were shocked and saddened at the news that the space shuttle *Challenger* exploded 73 seconds after liftoff, killing all seven of its crew members: Michael J. Smith, Dick Scobee, Ronald McNair, Ellison Onizuka, Christa McAuliffe, Gregory Jarvis, and Judith Resnik.

WORTH REPEATING

"Mr. Gorbachev, open this gate. Mr. Gorbachev, tear down this wall!"
—President Ronald Reagan, on June 12, 1987, challenging Soviet leader Mikhail Gorbachev to destroy the Berlin Wall

aid to anti-Communist movements in African, Asian, and Latin American countries that were supported by the Soviet Union.

Some historians give President Reagan a lot of credit for helping bring an end to the Cold War, but others believe the Soviet Union would have eventually collapsed on its own, which would have ended the Cold War. Others believe that both Reagan and Soviet leader Mikhail Gorbachev, who came to power in 1985, both helped end the Cold War.

There were many reasons for the end of the Soviet Union and the Cold War. In December 1991, more than two years after Ronald Reagan left office and was replaced by George H.W. Bush, the Soviet Union broke up into 15 separate countries. Americans—and people from around the world—celebrated the end of the Soviet Union and saw it as a victory for freedom.

The Cold War was now history, and the world—and America's place in it—had changed. Now there were no longer two military superpowers but just one: the United States. The world was still an uncertain, dangerous place, but the United States would no longer have to deal with its rival from the end of World War II.

The First Gulf War

Just before the end of the Cold War—and after the Soviet Union had stopped being a world military power—the United States found itself in a position where leadership was required during an international conflict.

The Persian Gulf War started on August 2, 1990, when Iraqi president Saddam Hussein ordered his forces to invade Kuwait and take control of the small, defenseless nation. Saddam ordered the invasion because he believed Kuwait was actually part of Iraq. He also believed that Kuwait's oil rigs near the border between the two countries had been siphoning off some of Iraq's oil supplies.

Saddam Hussein believed that the United States and other nations wouldn't come to Kuwait's defense, but he was wrong. Within days of the Iraqi invasion, the United States, as well as other members of the United Nations, demanded that Iraq immediately leave Kuwait. Not long after that, the United States and other UN member nations sent troops to

HISTORY MAKERS

H. Norman Schwarzkopf (born 1934), who is also known as "Stormin' Norman" and "The Bear," served as a US Army general and as commander of the Coalition Forces in the Persian Gulf War of 1991. Schwarzkopf had previously served in Vietnam and was promoted to the rank of general in 1988.

Saudi Arabia and other areas of the Persian Gulf region. This part of the war was called Operation Desert Shield.

On January 16, 1991—after Iraq refused to withdraw from Kuwait—a US-led coalition of UN nations began bombing Iraq and its forces in Kuwait. This part of the effort to liberate Kuwait was called Operation Desert Storm.

Saddam Hussein responded to the bombing by launching missiles (developed by the Soviet Union and known by the name Scud) at Israel

and Saudi Arabia. Saddam hoped that firing missiles at Israel would bring that nation into the war and cause other Arab nations to come to Iraq's defense. Just as Israel was set to retaliate against Iraq, President George H. W. Bush promised to protect Israel from the Scuds using US Patriot missiles, which shot down the Scuds.

By the time the Allied armies launched the ground war, the Iraqi forces in Kuwait were already beaten because the intense bombing campaign had cut off their supplies. Thousands of Iraqi soldiers in Kuwait, knowing the cause was hopeless, surrendered without a fight. Even when Iraq's Republican Guard, which was better trained and better equipped than other Iraqi forces, chose to fight, the Allies used better-quality American, British, and French equipment to quickly defeat them.

By February 26, 1991, the Allies had taken control of Kuwait City. Meanwhile, Allied forces chased the Iraqi army back toward the Iraq-Kuwait border. In southern Iraq, Allied forces gathered at the Euphrates River near Basra in southern Iraq, while rebellions against Saddam Hussein's government began. President Bush ordered a cease-fire on February 27, and the remaining Iraqi troops were allowed to return home. The fighting ended on March 3, 1991, when Iraq accepted the terms of the cease-fire.

President George H. W. Bush

The Close of the Twentieth Century

Though President George H. W. Bush led the Allies to victory over Iraq in the Persian Gulf War, the United States was going through an economic downturn during the last year of his term in office. That helped open the door to the election of the forty-second president of the United States, William Jefferson Clinton.

President Clinton won reelection in 1996 despite several scandals during his first term. That made him the first Democrat to serve two full terms as president since Franklin Delano Roosevelt more than 50 years earlier.

During Clinton's eight years in office, the United States enjoyed strong economic growth. In 1993 he signed the Family and Medical Leave Act, which required businesses who employed a large number of people to allow their employees unpaid leave when they had family or medical emergencies. Also, he worked with Republicans, who took control of the House of Representatives and the Senate in 1994, to reduce the nation's budget deficit. In 1999 the government ran on a balanced budget (meaning it didn't spend more than it took in through taxes) for the first time since 1969. ✖

President Bill Clinton

CHAPTER 9

History Still in the Making

The Start of the Twenty-first Century

The 1990s were a relatively peaceful and prosperous time for most Americans (though there were a few international conflicts along the way). But as 1999 turned to 2000 (Y2K, as some people call it), things quickly became more uncertain for many Americans.

The first decade of the new millennium featured some unique historic events for the United States, including a presidential election that wasn't decided for weeks after the vote was taken, a horrible attack on our home soil by terrorists, two long wars, and the election of the first African American president of the United States.

A lot of the history that took place during that decade is still being written as historians debate the importance and meaning of these events. In this chapter, you'll read about the events and people that made the most recent decade in US history so memorable.

An Unforgettable Presidential Election

The US presidential election of 2000 pitted Democrat Al Gore, the vice president of the United States and a former senator from Tennessee, against Republican George W. Bush, governor of Texas and the son of former president George H. W. Bush. The candidates were running to replace Bill Clinton, the forty-second president of the United States, who had served the maximum allowed two terms.

The 2000 presidential election made history for a lot of reasons. First of all, it was the closest election since 1876, when Rutherford B. Hayes was named the winner over Samuel J. Tilden in an election historians still dispute. Bush won the election with 271 electoral votes to Gore's 266.

Al Gore   George W. Bush

Second, it was only the fourth presidential election—and the first since 1888, when Republican Benjamin Harrison defeated the president in office, Democrat Grover Cleveland—in which a candidate won the electoral vote without winning the popular vote (Gore received 543,895 more votes than Bush nationwide).

Historically, most close elections are followed by accusations of fraud and disputes over vote counts. The 2000 presidential election was no exception. In fact, it was one of the most bitterly disputed elections in US history.

What Happened on November 7, 2000. . .and Beyond

The presidential election of 2000 was close throughout, so close that it came down to one state—Florida—and a few hundred votes separating the candidates. Whoever won Florida would also win the election.

Early in the evening of that Election Day, the Associated Press, based on several factors, declared Vice President Gore the winner in Florida. The major news networks around the nation agreed with the AP and also declared Gore the winner. But just a few hours after that declaration, the vote count in Florida tightened, and it no longer looked certain that Gore was the winner. Not long after that, the networks began retracting their projection that Gore had won and started calling the election "too close to call."

By the wee hours of the morning on November 8, some estimates had Bush pulling ahead of Gore by 50,000 votes. The news networks began projecting Bush as the winner, and Gore called Bush to concede the election. But less than an hour after Gore's call, his advisers told him that Bush's lead had shrunk to less than 1,000 votes. So Gore called Bush again and took back his concession. Not long after that, the networks retracted their projection that Bush had won and again declared the election "too close to call."

By the morning of November 8, all the votes in Florida had been counted, and Bush appeared to be the winner with 1,784 more votes than Gore. But some people said there were problems with the votes in some areas of Florida, leading to more doubt about the outcome. Also, due to Florida law, the election results could not be certified (made official) until after a full recount of the votes.

What followed over the next five weeks was a series of legal challenges and lawsuits—some going all the way to the US Supreme Court. People who supported Bush claimed that the Gore campaign was trying to "steal" the election by requesting recounts in heavily Democratic counties, while Gore supporters accused the Bush campaign of trying to win by keeping some votes from being counted.

Finally, on Wednesday, December 13, Al Gore ran out of legal options. He was still behind in the Florida vote count, so he went on national television to tell the American people that he had accepted Bush's victory in the election. Bush responded by promising that he would work to reconcile a nation that had been deeply divided over the Florida election results.

On January 20, George Bush was sworn in as the forty-third president of the United States. Bush was reelected in 2004 and served eight years as president.

WORTH REPEATING

"God is not on the side of any nation, yet we know He is on the side of justice. Our finest moments have come when we faithfully serve the cause of justice for our own citizens, and for the people of other lands."
—George W. Bush

September 11: A Dark Day in American History

When someone mentions certain dates in history, you know which historic event they're talking about. September 11, 2001, is one of those dates. When someone says "September 11" or "9/11," you know they're talking about one of the worst days in American history.

Early that morning, nineteen hijackers from a terrorist group called al-Qaeda hijacked four commercial airliners and began using them as weapons against targets inside the United States.

At 8:46 a.m. Eastern Time, one of those groups of hijackers crashed American Airlines Flight 11 into the World Trade Center's North Tower in New York City. Less than 20 minutes later, United Airlines flight 175 hit the South Tower. Both buildings collapsed less than two hours later.

At 9:37 a.m., another group of hijackers flew American Airlines Flight 77 into the Pentagon, the headquarters for the United States Department of Defense, which is located in Arlington, Virginia, not far from Washington, DC. At 10:03 a.m., the fourth flight, United Airlines Flight 93, crashed in a field near Shanksville, Pennsylvania, after passengers on board learned of the other attacks through telephone calls and fought back against the hijackers.

It's not certain what target the hijackers intended to hit with Flight 93, but it is thought that they wanted to hit the US Capitol Building (where Congress meets) or the White House, where the president lives.

A Strong Response

In the days following the September 11 attacks, the United States worked to find out who was responsible. Once the United States and international intelligence knew beyond a doubt that al-Qaeda had carried out the attacks, the United States began an anti-terrorism campaign against

Afghanistan—actually the Afghan government, the Taliban—which had allowed terrorist leader Osama bin Laden and al-Qaeda to live and train there.

On October 7, 2001—less than one month after the September 11 terrorist attacks, the United States military, along with British armed forces, launched Operation Enduring Freedom, a campaign to find Osama bin Laden, to end al-Qaeda's use of Afghanistan as a base for worldwide terrorist operations, to remove the Taliban from power, and to help the Afghan people create a new government.

The first phase of Operation Enduring Freedom was over in a matter of weeks. Soldiers from the Afghan United Front, which had opposed the Taliban, worked with American and British forces to drive the Taliban out of power. The operation was also aided by massive air support from the United States.

Within three months after September 11, all of the major Taliban-controlled cities had fallen to the United States and its allies. Many people thought the war was nearly over. But bin Laden and other top al-Qaeda leaders fled the country. The United States continued to search for Osama bin Laden until May 1, 2011, when a team of Navy Seals stormed a compound in Abbottabad, Pakistan, and shot and killed him.

Most of the Taliban's top leaders left Afghanistan and fled to neighboring Pakistan. The Islamic Republic of Afghanistan was established with a temporary government under the leadership of Hamid Karzai. In 2004 the Afghan people voted to keep Karzai's government in power.

In 2003 Taliban forces, which were stationed in Pakistan, attempted to fight back against Karzai's government and against international troops in Afghanistan. Since 2006 the Afghan people have suffered as Taliban-led terrorists increased their operations in Afghanistan. When the US war in Afghanistan began, many people thought it wouldn't last long. But in June of 2010, the Afghan war surpassed the Vietnam War of the 1960s and 1970s as America's longest war.

The Second War with Iraq

In 2003 the United States went to war with Iraq again. President Bush and British Prime Minister Tony Blair believed Iraq was making dangerous weapons, called "weapons of mass destruction" (or WMD), which they saw as threats to the other nations around the world. They also believed there were connections between Iraq and al-Qaeda and that if Iraq were to develop WMDs, they could end up in the hands of terrorists. The Iraq War, which is also called the Second Gulf War or Operation Iraqi Freedom, began on March 20, 2003. Troops from the United States and from the United Kingdom invaded Iraq for the purpose of removing President Saddam Hussein from power.

HISTORIC HAPPENINGS

On October 26, 2001, President George W. Bush signed the Patriot Act, which gave law enforcement officers in the United States more authority to search telephone and e-mail communications, as well as medical, financial, and other records. It also gave authorities in law enforcement and immigration more authority to arrest and send home immigrants who were suspected of acts of terrorism.

Statues of Saddam Hussein

The Iraq War started early in the morning on March 19, 2003, when American planes dropped bombs and the US Navy fired missiles at key targets in and near the Iraqi capital city of Baghdad. The initial attack was followed by an air assault against southern Iraqi targets. Iraq answered with missile attacks on US military positions in the Kuwaiti desert.

On April 3, after three weeks of furious fighting, American forces reached Saddam International Airport, located on the outskirts of Baghdad, and two days later US armed forces entered Baghdad and began a series of raids that lasted for several days. On April 9, the US-led coalition extended its control over the city of Baghdad. That day American soldiers helped Iraqi crowds tear down a large statue of Saddam Hussein.

Mission Accomplished?

On May 1, 2003, President Bush boarded the aircraft carrier USS *Abraham Lincoln*, which was operating a few miles west of San Diego, California, and delivered the now well-known "Mission Accomplished" speech. In that speech, he declared that major combat in Iraq had ended.

HISTORIC HAPPENINGS

On the morning of Monday, August 19, 2005, Hurricane Katrina, one of the strongest hurricanes in recorded history, slammed into the Gulf Coast area of the United States. At least 1,863 people died as a result of the storm and the floods that followed, making it the deadliest hurricane to hit the United States since 1928. The storm also did $81 billion in damage. New Orleans, Louisiana, suffered the highest number of deaths in the storm as 80 percent of the city was flooded.

But even though the United States and its allies had thoroughly defeated Iraq's military forces, it turned out that the war was far from over.

On July 22, troops from the US 101st Airborne Division killed Udai and Qusay Hussein, the sons of Saddam Hussein. On December 13, Saddam Hussein was captured. Later the Iraqi government put him on trial and executed him for war crimes.

Even though President Bush had announced that major combat missions in Iraq had ended, and even though Saddam Hussein had been captured, the United States military remained in Iraq for several more years, battling different groups that wanted the Americans to leave Iraq.

After President Bush's "Mission Accomplished" speech, forces from the United States and its allies began to notice an increase in attacks in different regions of Iraq. Anti-American fighters in those areas used mortars, missiles, suicide attacks, car bombs, small arms fire, improvised explosive devices (also called IED's), and rocket-propelled grenades to inflict casualties.

Saddam Hussein

139

As US casualties from these attacks mounted, the American public stopped supporting the war—especially after no weapons of mass destruction were found in Iraq—and President Bush's popularity began to decline.

A National Change of Course

In the 2006 elections—which were called "midterm elections" because the next presidential election wasn't until 2008—President Bush's political party, the Republicans, lost badly to the Democrats, who took a 233–202 advantage in the House of Representatives and forged a 49–49 tie in the United States Senate (two independents, Bernie Sanders of Vermont and Joe Lieberman of Connecticut, were also elected, and both sided with the Democrats most of the time).

After the 2006 elections, the war in Iraq continued, and many people believe the war played a part in what happened during the 2008 presidential election.

Another Historic Election

On February 10, 2007, Barack Obama, then serving as a senator from the state of Illinois, announced that he would run for president of the United States. On August 27, 2008, after a long season of campaigning against other Democrats for the right to represent the party as their candidate, Obama was

John McCain and Sarah Palin

Barack Obama

declared the Democratic Party's nominee, making him the first African American in history to run on a major party ticket.

As George W. Bush's second term as president was drawing to a close, things weren't looking good for his party, the Republicans. The US military was mired in two wars and the national economy wasn't performing as well as people wanted it to. Making things worse for the Republicans, in 2008 the American economy slid into the deepest recession since the Great Depression. Many people wondered if the United States was seeing a replay of the 1929 stock market crash and the Great Depression that followed.

Historically, when the United States economy is in trouble, it spells doom for the political party in control of things. Even though George W. Bush had served two terms and would be leaving office, people still associated the nation's economic problems with his party. It was going to be an uphill battle for the Republican candidate, John McCain—one he wouldn't win.

On November 4, 2008, Barack Obama defeated McCain in the presidential election, making Obama the first African American to win election as president of the United States.

HISTORIC HAPPENINGS

On September 29, 2008, the Dow Jones Industrial Average (a system that tracks a wide variety of stocks for investors), suffered through its worst single-day point loss ever when it fell more than 777 points. On October 15, it fell by another 733 points. Even though a lot of people lost money on those days, they weren't the worst days for the stock market. On October 19, 1987, the Dow Jones Industrial Average fell more than 22 percent in one day.

A Big Change at the Top. . .and Other Places

After Barack Obama was sworn into office as the forty-fourth president of the United States in January 2009, many people who had supported him during his campaign hoped he would move the country in a completely different direction than Bush had.

Adding to that hope was the fact that other Democratic candidates had won major victories in the election. Before the 2008 election, the US House of Representatives was made up of 235 Democrats and 199 Republicans. After the election, the number of Democrats had grown to 257 seats, and the Republicans now had only178 seats in the House. The Democrats also made big gains in the Senate.

Many of President Obama's supporters believed the country should immediately withdraw from the wars in Afghanistan and Iraq, that the Patriot Act should not be renewed, that the government should provide all people with health insurance, that wealthy Americans should pay more of their income in taxes, and that the government should do a lot more to protect the environment.

In late February 2009, President Obama announced that he wanted to withdraw US combat troops from Iraq within 18 months, but that he would leave about 50,000 troops in the country "to advise and train Iraqi security forces and to provide intelligence and surveillance." On August 31, 2010, Obama delivered a speech from the Oval Office and told the American people that "the American combat mission in Iraq has ended. Operation Iraqi Freedom is over, and the Iraqi people now have lead responsibility for the security of their country."

When President Obama first took office, people who agreed with his positions on those and other issues hoped he would take advantage of the Democrats' big advantage in Congress to pass laws they liked. On the other side though, people who thought President Obama wanted to do too much and make government too big feared that the Democratic advantage in Congress would mean there would be no "checks and balances"—meaning Obama would too easily help pass laws the other side disagreed with.

President Obama's Big Victory

In March 2010, President Obama used his advantage in Congress to help pass the Patient Protection and Affordable Care Act and the Health Care and Education Reconciliation Act of 2010. These two bills together made up what is called health care reform.

Polls of American voters showed that both bills were very unpopular, but they passed in Congress—the Senate on December 24, 2009 and the House of Representatives on March 21, 2010—without a single yes vote from the Republican side. In the final House vote, 178 Republicans and 34 Democrats voted against the bill, which narrowly passed.

After the bill's passage, it was challenged legally on the basis that some parts of the law are unconstitutional. Many or most of the legal challenges came from a part of the legislation that requires all citizens of the United States to have health insurance. Supporters of the mandate said that it would help drive health insurance costs down, but those who opposed it said it would violate individual Americans' personal liberties. More than half of the 50 states filed lawsuits in hopes of overturning the individual mandate section of the law. ❎

CHAPTER 10

Where Do We Go from Here?

Though this book is almost complete, history continues.

Halfway through Barack Obama's presidency, in the 2010 "midterm" election, American voters changed the makeup of Congress—putting the House of Representatives back under Republican control and cutting the Democrats' lead in the Senate.

By 2012, when this book was printed, many politicians were hoping to run against Obama in the 2012 election. American soldiers continued to serve in dangerous places around the world. The national economy continued to struggle, as politicians argued over taxes and government spending.

Maybe all the uncertainty in the world makes you uncomfortable. Maybe some important people in your life are worried or out of work or wondering what big event will happen next—and what it will mean to all of us as Americans.

Where do we go from here? Only God knows. But never forget that He's in control!

Appendix A: The Presidents of the United States of America

George Washington, 1789–1797

John Adams, 1797–1801

Thomas Jefferson, 1801–1809

James Madison, 1809–1817

James Monroe, 1817–1825

John Quincy Adams, 1825–1829

Andrew Jackson, 1829–1837

Martin Van Buren, 1837–1841

William Henry Harrison, 1841

John Tyler, 1841–1845

James K. Polk, 1845–1849

Zachary Taylor, 1849–1850

Millard Fillmore, 1850–1853

Franklin Pierce, 1853–1857

James Buchanan, 1857–1861

Abraham Lincoln, 1861–1865

Andrew Johnson, 1865–1869

Ulysses S. Grant, 1869–1877

Rutherford B. Hayes, 1877–1881

James A. Garfield, 1881

Chester A. Arthur, 1881–1885

Grover Cleveland, 1885–1889

Benjamin Harrison, 1889–1893

Grover Cleveland, 1893–1897

William McKinley, 1897–1901

Theodore Roosevelt, 1901–1909

William Howard Taft, 1909–1913

Woodrow Wilson, 1913–1921

Warren G. Harding, 1921–1923

Calvin Coolidge, 1923–1929

Herbert Hoover, 1929–1933

Franklin D. Roosevelt, 1933–1945

Harry S Truman, 1945–1953

Dwight D. Eisenhower, 1953–1961

John F. Kennedy, 1961–1963

Lyndon B. Johnson, 1963–1969

Richard M. Nixon, 1969–1974

Gerald R. Ford, 1974–1977

James E. "Jimmy" Carter, 1977–1981

Ronald Reagan, 1981–1989

George H. W. Bush, 1989–1993

William J. Clinton, 1993–2001

George W. Bush, 2001–2009

Barack Obama, 2009–

Appendix B: The Declaration of Independence

IN CONGRESS, July 4, 1776.

The Unanimous Declaration of the Thirteen United States of America

When in the course of human events, it becomes necessary for one people to dissolve the political bands which have connected them with another, and to assume among the powers of the earth, the separate and equal station to which the Laws of Nature and of Nature's God entitle them, a decent respect to the opinions of mankind requires that they should declare the causes which impel them to the separation.

We hold these truths to be self-evident, that all men are created equal, that they are endowed by their Creator with certain unalienable Rights, that among these are Life, Liberty and the pursuit of Happiness.

That to secure these rights, Governments are instituted among Men, deriving their just powers from the consent of the governed.

That whenever any Form of Government becomes destructive of these ends, it is the Right of the People to alter or to abolish it, and to institute new Government, laying its foundation on such principles and organizing its powers in such form, as to them shall seem most likely to effect their Safety and Happiness. Prudence, indeed, will dictate that Governments long established should not be changed for light and transient causes; and accordingly all experience hath shewn that mankind are more disposed to suffer, while evils are sufferable, than to right themselves by abolishing the forms to which they are accustomed. But when a long train of abuses and usurpations, pursuing invariably the same Object evinces a design to reduce them under absolute Despotism, it is their right, it is their duty, to throw off such Government, and to provide new Guards for their future security.

Such has been the patient sufferance of these Colonies; and such is now the necessity which constrains them to alter their former Systems of Government. The history of the present King of Great Britain is a history of repeated injuries and usurpations, all having in direct object the establishment of an absolute Tyranny over these States. To prove this, let Facts be submitted to a candid world.

He has refused his Assent to Laws, the most wholesome and necessary for the public good.

He has forbidden his Governors to pass Laws of immediate and pressing importance, unless suspended in their operation till his Assent should be obtained; and when so suspended, he has utterly neglected to attend to them.

He has refused to pass other Laws for the accommodation of large districts of people, unless those people would relinquish the right of Representation in the Legislature, a right inestimable to them and formidable to tyrants only.

He has called together legislative bodies at places unusual, uncomfortable, and distant from the depository of their public Records, for the sole purpose of fatiguing them into compliance with his measures.

He has dissolved Representative Houses repeatedly, for opposing with manly firmness his invasions on the rights of the people.

He has refused for a long time, after such dissolutions, to cause others to be elected; whereby the Legislative powers, incapable of Annihilation, have returned to the People at large for their exercise; the State remaining in the meantime exposed to all the dangers of invasion from without, and convulsions within.

He has endeavored to prevent the population of these States; for that purpose obstructing the Laws for Naturalization of Foreigners; refusing to pass others to encourage their migrations hither, and raising the conditions of new Appropriations of Lands.

He has obstructed the Administration of Justice, by refusing his Assent to Laws for establishing Judiciary powers.

He has made Judges dependent on his Will alone, for the tenure of their offices, and the amount and payment of their salaries.

He has erected a multitude of New Offices, and sent hither swarms of Officers to harass our people, and eat out their substance.

He has kept among us, in times of peace, Standing Armies without the Consent of our legislatures.

He has affected to render the Military independent of and superior to the Civil power.

He has combined with others to subject us to a jurisdiction foreign to our constitution, and unacknowledged by our laws; giving his Assent to their Acts of pretended Legislation:

For Quartering large bodies of armed troops among us:

For protecting them, by a mock Trial, from punishment for any Murders which they should commit on the Inhabitants of these States:

For cutting off our Trade with all parts of the world:

For imposing Taxes on us without our Consent:

For depriving us in many cases, of the benefits of Trial by Jury:

For transporting us beyond Seas to be tried for pretended offences:

For abolishing the free System of English Laws in a neighboring Province, establishing therein an Arbitrary government, and enlarging its Boundaries so as to render it at once an example and fit instrument for introducing the same absolute rule into these Colonies:

For taking away our Charters, abolishing our most valuable Laws, and altering fundamentally the Forms of our Governments:

For suspending our own Legislatures, and declaring themselves invested with power to legislate for us in all cases whatsoever.

He has abdicated Government here, by declaring us out of his Protection and waging War against us.

He has plundered our seas, ravaged our Coasts, burnt our towns, and destroyed the lives of our people.

He is at this time transporting large Armies of foreign Mercenaries to complete the works of death, desolation and tyranny, already begun with circumstances of Cruelty & perfidy scarcely paralleled in the most barbarous ages, and totally unworthy the Head of a civilized nation.

He has constrained our fellow Citizens taken Captive on the high Seas to bear Arms against their Country, to become the executioners of their friends and Brethren, or to fall themselves by their Hands.

He has excited domestic insurrections amongst us, and has endeavored to bring on the inhabitants of our frontiers, the merciless Indian Savages, whose known rule of warfare, is an undistinguished destruction of all ages, sexes and conditions.

In every stage of these Oppressions We have Petitioned for Redress in the most humble terms: Our repeated Petitions have been answered only by repeated injury. A Prince whose character is thus marked by every act which may define a Tyrant, is unfit to be the ruler of a free people.

Nor have We been wanting in attentions to our British brethren. We have warned them from time to time of attempts by their legislature to extend an unwarrantable jurisdiction over us. We have reminded them of the circumstances of our emigration and settlement here. We have appealed to their native justice and magnanimity, and we have conjured them by the ties of our common kindred to disavow these usurpations, which would inevitably interrupt our connections and correspondence. They too have been deaf to the voice of justice and of consanguinity. We must, therefore, acquiesce in the necessity, which denounces our Separation, and hold them, as we hold the rest of mankind, Enemies in War, in Peace Friends.

We, therefore, the Representatives of the United States of America, in General Congress, Assembled, appealing to the Supreme Judge of the world for the rectitude of our intentions, do, in the Name, and by Authority of the good People of these Colonies, solemnly publish and declare, That these United Colonies are, and of Right ought to be Free and Independent States; that they are Absolved from all Allegiance to the British Crown, and that all political connection between them and the State of Great Britain, is and ought to be totally dissolved; and that as Free and Independent States, they have full Power to levy War, conclude Peace, contract Alliances, establish Commerce, and to do all other Acts and Things which Independent States may of right do. And for the support of this Declaration, with a firm reliance on the protection of divine Providence, we mutually pledge to each other our Lives, our Fortunes and our sacred Honor. ✖

Appendix C: Abraham Lincoln's Gettysburg Address

Fourscore and seven years ago our fathers brought forth on this continent a new nation, conceived in liberty and dedicated to the proposition that all men are created equal.

Now we are engaged in a great civil war, testing whether that nation, or any nation so conceived and so dedicated, can long endure. We are met on a great battlefield of that war. We have come to dedicate a portion of that field as a final resting place for those who here gave their lives that that nation might live. It is altogether fitting and proper that we should do this. But, in a larger sense, we cannot dedicate, we cannot consecrate, we cannot hallow this ground. The brave men, living and dead, who struggled here have consecrated it far above our poor power to add or detract. The world will little note, nor long remember what we say here, but it can never forget what they did here. It is for us the living, rather, to be dedicated here to the unfinished work which they who fought here have thus far so nobly advanced. It is rather for us to be here dedicated to the great task remaining before us—that from these honored dead we take increased devotion to that cause for which they gave the last full measure of devotion—that we here highly resolve that these dead shall not have died in vain—that this nation shall have a new birth of freedom and that government of the people, by the people, for the people, shall not perish from the earth.

Appendix D: Martin Luther King Jr.'s "I Have a Dream" Speech

I am happy to join with you today in what will go down in history as the greatest demonstration for freedom in the history of our nation.

Five score years ago, a great American, in whose symbolic shadow we stand today, signed the Emancipation Proclamation. This momentous decree came as a great beacon light of hope to millions of Negro slaves who had been seared in the flames of withering injustice. It came as a joyous daybreak to end the long night of their captivity.

But one hundred years later, the Negro still is not free. One hundred years later, the life of the Negro is still sadly crippled by the manacles of segregation and the chains of discrimination. One hundred years later, the Negro lives on a lonely island of poverty in the midst of a vast ocean of material prosperity. One hundred years later, the Negro is still languishing in the corners of American society and finds himself an exile in his own land. So we have come here today to dramatize a shameful condition.

In a sense we have come to our nation's capital to cash a check. When the architects of our republic wrote the magnificent words of the Constitution and the Declaration of Independence, they were signing a promissory note to which every American was to fall heir. This note was a promise that all men, yes, black men as well as white men, would be guaranteed the unalienable rights of life, liberty, and the pursuit of happiness.

It is obvious today that America has defaulted on this promissory note insofar as her citizens of color are concerned. Instead of honoring this sacred obligation, America has given the Negro people a bad check, a check which has come back marked "insufficient funds." But we refuse to believe that the bank of justice is bankrupt. We refuse to believe that there are insufficient funds in the great vaults of opportunity of this nation. So we have come to cash this check—a check that will give us upon demand the riches of freedom and the security of justice. We have also come to this hallowed spot to remind America of the fierce urgency of now. This is no time to engage in the luxury of cooling off or to take the tranquilizing drug of gradualism.

Now is the time to make real the promises of democracy. Now is the time to rise from the dark and desolate valley of segregation to the sunlit path of racial justice. Now is the time to lift our nation from the quick sands of racial injustice to the solid rock of brotherhood. Now is the time to make justice a reality for all of God's children.

It would be fatal for the nation to overlook the urgency of the moment. This sweltering summer of the Negro's legitimate discontent will not pass until there is an invigorating autumn of freedom and equality. Nineteen sixty-three is not an end, but a beginning. Those who hope that the Negro needed to blow off steam and will now be content will have a rude awakening if the nation returns to business as usual. There will be neither rest nor tranquility in America until the Negro is granted his citizenship rights. The whirlwinds of revolt will continue to shake the foundations of our nation until the bright day of justice emerges.

But there is something that I must say to my people who stand on the warm threshold which leads into the palace of justice. In the process of gaining our rightful place we must not be guilty of wrongful deeds. Let us not seek to satisfy our thirst for freedom by drinking from the cup of bitterness and hatred.

We must forever conduct our struggle on the high plane of dignity and discipline. We must not allow our creative protest to degenerate into physical violence. Again and again we must rise to the majestic heights of meeting physical force with soul force. The marvelous new militancy which has engulfed the Negro community must not lead us to a distrust of all white people, for many of our white brothers, as evidenced by their presence here today, have come to realize that their destiny is tied up with our destiny. They have come to realize that their freedom is inextricably bound to our freedom. We cannot walk alone.

As we walk, we must make the pledge that we shall always march ahead. We cannot turn back. There are those who are asking the devotees of civil rights, "When will you be satisfied?" We can never be satisfied as long as the Negro is the victim of the unspeakable horrors of police brutality. We can never be satisfied, as long as our bodies, heavy with the fatigue of travel, cannot gain lodging in the motels of the highways and the hotels of the cities. We cannot be satisfied as long as the Negro's basic mobility is from a smaller ghetto to a larger one. We can never be satisfied as long as our children are stripped of their selfhood and robbed of their dignity by signs stating "For Whites Only". We cannot be satisfied as long as a Negro in Mississippi cannot vote and a Negro in New York believes he has nothing for which to vote. No, no, we are not satisfied, and we will not be satisfied until justice rolls down like waters and righteousness like a mighty stream.

I am not unmindful that some of you have come here out of great trials and tribulations. Some of you have come fresh from narrow jail cells. Some of you have come from areas where your quest for freedom left you battered by the storms of persecution and staggered by the winds of police brutality. You have been the veterans of creative suffering. Continue to work with the faith that unearned suffering is redemptive.

Go back to Mississippi, go back to Alabama, go back to South Carolina, go back to Georgia, go back to Louisiana, go back to the slums and ghettos of our northern cities, knowing that somehow this situation can and will be changed. Let us not wallow in the valley of despair.

I say to you today, my friends, so even though we face the difficulties of today and tomorrow, I still have a dream. It is a dream deeply rooted in the American dream.

I have a dream that one day this nation will rise up and live out the true meaning of its creed: "We hold these truths to be self evident: that all men are created equal."

I have a dream that one day on the red hills of Georgia the sons of former slaves and the sons of former slave owners will be able to sit down together at the table of brotherhood.

I have a dream that one day even the state of Mississippi, a state sweltering with the heat of injustice, sweltering with the heat of oppression, will be transformed into an oasis of freedom and justice.

I have a dream that my four little children will one day live in a nation where they will not be judged by the color of their skin but by the content of their character.

I have a dream today.

I have a dream that one day, down in Alabama, with its vicious racists, with its governor having his lips dripping with the words of interposition and nullification; one day right there in Alabama, little black boys and black girls will be able to join hands with little white boys and white girls as sisters and brothers.

I have a dream today.

I have a dream that one day every valley shall be exalted, every hill and mountain shall be made low, the rough places will be made plain, and the crooked places will be made straight, and the glory of the Lord shall be revealed, and all flesh shall see it together.

This is our hope. This is the faith that I go back to the South with. With this faith we will be able to hew out of the mountain of despair a stone of hope. With this faith we will be able to transform the jangling discords of our nation into a beautiful symphony of brotherhood. With this faith we will be able to work together, to pray together, to struggle together, to go to jail together, to stand up for freedom together, knowing that we will be free one day.

This will be the day when all of God's children will be able to sing with a new meaning, "My country, 'tis of thee, sweet land of liberty, of thee I sing. Land where my fathers died, land of the pilgrim's pride, from every mountainside, let freedom ring."

And if America is to be a great nation this must become true. So let freedom ring from the prodigious hilltops of New Hampshire. Let freedom ring from the mighty mountains of New York. Let freedom ring from the heightening Alleghenies of Pennsylvania!

Let freedom ring from the snowcapped Rockies of Colorado!

Let freedom ring from the curvaceous slopes of California!

But not only that; let freedom ring from Stone Mountain of Georgia!

Let freedom ring from Lookout Mountain of Tennessee!

Let freedom ring from every hill and molehill of Mississippi. From every mountainside, let freedom ring.

And when this happens, when we allow freedom to ring, when we let it ring from every village and every hamlet, from every state and every city, we will be able to speed up that day when all of God's children, black men and white men, Jews and Gentiles, Protestants and Catholics, will be able to join hands and sing in the words of the old Negro spiritual, "Free at last! free at last! thank God Almighty, we are free at last!"

Key: IS=iStockphoto; SS=Shutterstock; WM=Wikimedia

7 SS; 9 ship: SS; forest: SS/Songquan Deng; 10 SS/Alex Balako; 11 stamp: SS/Magnolia; 12–13 IS/dlerick; 14 SS/Fanny Reno; 15 SS/LesPalenik; 16 WM/Jonathan Snyder; 18 WM/SteamFan ; 19 WM/Paul van Somer; 20 WM; 21 SS/Rob Byron ; 22 WM; 23 SS/Israel Mckee; 24 Mayflower Compact: WM; ship: SS/Stephen Coburn; 26–27 SS/Kenneth V. Pilon; 29 WM; 30 SS/Danny Xu; 31 glass blowing: SS/Zina Seletskaya; spool: SS/Garsya; 32 Liberty Bell: SS/Edwin Verin; flags : SS/Diego Barbieri; 33 coins: SS/Tatiana Popova; 34 sugar bag: SS/buriy; Stamp act: WM; 35 SS/Caitlin Mirra; 36 WM; 37 SS/Jeffrey M. Frank; 38–39 WM; 40 SS/Gregory Gerber; 42 SS/John Kwan; 43 SS/Susan Law Cain; 45 WM; 46 SS/Liudmila Cherniak; 50 signing of Constitution: WM; George Washington: SS/pandapaw; 53 map: SS/Maximus256; mountains: SS/Julie Lubick; 54 SS/Jose Gil; 55 SS/Kenneth Graff; 57 SS/Sue Smith; 58 SS/picsbyst; 60 SS/J.T. Lewis; 61 SS/Trinacria Photo; 62 SS/Antonio Abrignani; 63 SS; 64 SS/Steve Estvanik; 66 SS/lkphotographers; 69 flags: SS/Peteri; battle: SS/Steve Estvanik; 71 SS/Antonio Abrignani; 72–73 SS/David W. Leindecker; 74 SS/akva; 75 SS/Jorge Moro; 76 WM; 78 SS/zulufoto; 79 WM; 80 WM/Wknight94; 82–83 SS/pandapaw; 84 SS/zentilia; 85 Statue of Liberty: SS/Edwin Verin; Uncle Sam: WM; 86 WM; 87 WM; 88–89 SS/Norman Pogson; 90 SS/tale; 91 phonograph: SS/Lebedinski Vladislav; telephone: SS/Holly Kuchera; barbed wire: SS/Dmitriy Shironosov; Wright Flyer/WM; 92 WM; 94 WM; 95 SS/Derek Jensen; 96 WM; 97 SS/Tim Mainiero; 99 SS/Len Green; 100 WM; 101 WM; 103 SS/dalmingo; 104–105 SS/Dwight Smith; 106 SS/Tupungato; 107 Nazi flag: SS/Jim Vallee; white flag: SS/Alfonso de Tomas; 108 WM; 109 SS/Norman Chan; 110 SS/ruskpp; 111 WM; 113 SS/Alan Freed; 114 WM; 115 SS/Sundebo; 116 Civil Rights march: WM; Vietnam: WM; 117 SS/JustASC; 118 SS/MWaits; 119 WM/Jeffrey Rohan; 120 SS/Nickolay Stanev; 121 WM/NASA; 122 Aldrin on moon: WM/NASA; Neil Armstrong: WM; 123 Nixon: WM/Ollie Atkins; Watergate: SS/Vsevolod33; 125 WM; 126 WM; 127 Saddam Hussein: WM; jet: WM/Senior Airman Chris Putnam, USAF; 128 WM/PHC Holmes; 129 WM; 130 WM; 131 WM: Mario Roberto Durán Ortiz 132 Al Gore: SS/jaimaa; President George W. Bush: SS/Christopher Halloran; 133 SS/Lisa F. Young; 134 SS/Ken Tannenbaum; 135 SS/Larry Bruce; 136 SS/Carolina K. Smith, M.D.; 137 SS/Jim Gordon, CIV; 138 SS/Marcio Jose Bastos Silva; 139 flood: SS/Caitlin Mirra; Saddam Hussein: WM; 140 John McCain and Sarah Palin: SS/R. Gino Santa Maria; Barack Obama: SS/Russell Shively; 143SS/Albert de Bruijn; 144–150 all WM